Adrian Searle was born on the Isle of Wight in 1949, and is a member of a long-established Island family. He has worked as a journalist for 23 years and is a former editor of the *Isle of Wight Weekly Post*. A keen student of 'all things Wight', he has written a number of articles and books on various aspects of the Island's history, including *Isle of Wight at War 1939-1945*. He now lives in St Helens.

Following page
Bembridge Windmill.
[see Walk 13]

Walking
ISLE OF WIGHT
HISTORY
Adrian Searle

THE DOVECOTE PRESS

First published in 2004 by
The Dovecote Press Ltd
Stanbridge, Wimborne, Dorset BH21 4JD

ISBN 1 904349 31 5

Printed and bound by The Baskerville Press, Salisbury, Wiltshire

All papers used by The Dovecote Press are natural, recyclable products
made from wood grown in sustainable, well-managed forests.

A CIP catalogue record for this book is available
from the British Library

1 3 5 7 9 8 6 4 2

Contents

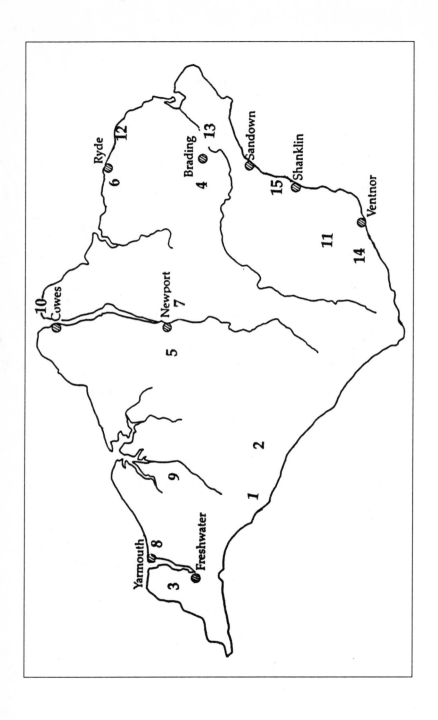

Introduction

It's not stretching things too far to describe the Isle of Wight as a walkers' paradise. The Island is criss-crossed with more than 500 miles of well-maintained, clearly signposted and numbered footpaths. The Coastal Path alone skirts 30 miles of the often spectacular Heritage Coastline. Other paths weave through atmospheric woodlands, follow the routes of ancient trackways across glorious open countryside, climb the high chalk downs and descend as hollow-ways through steep-banked cuttings. Quiet, pretty rural lanes, largely undisturbed by motor traffic, add a further dimension to the walking experience. More than half of the Isle of Wight is designated an Area of Outstanding Natural Beauty. It's little wonder that, each May, the Island hosts what is now the UK's largest walking festival.

Add to all that the rich vein of history that runs beneath each step of the many walking routes and the Isle of Wight is revealed as the ideal setting for a book of this nature. Dinosaur Island. Roman Vectis. Medieval battleground. The Victorian seaside presided over by Queen Victoria herself. The variety and wealth of Wight's historical legacy is astonishing for such a small offshore area of land. In many ways, it is a microcosm of the history of England. In others, it is markedly distinctive.

This book rolls into one the key elements of the Isle of Wight's geography and history. Collectively, the 15 walks cover the north, south, east, west and heart of the Island, and each has a different historical theme. The walks also offer a wide choice of terrain and length, ranging from the easy to the demanding – and just about every category in between. All are visually and historically rewarding. Roads – those that *do* carry significant traffic – have been avoided wherever possible.

The evidence of history abounds in the Island. Prehistory, too. The first walk in the book takes you to the headland above the Pine Raft, the fossilised remains of trees millions of years old. From there, the walks are arranged chronologically, according to the historical theme. The adoption of themes does not mean the other points of historical interest along the routes – from whichever period – are neglected. It would make little sense, for example, to ignore the subsequent medieval development of Brading – when the evidence of that period is so conspicuously obvious – in describing the route of a walk themed around the capture and occupation of the Isle of Wight by the Romans.

Out in the countryside, there's always a good chance of encountering the Island's wildlife. Some walks pass through, or close to, nature reserves – including the route at out-of-the-way Newtown, which provides access to the hide from where you can observe the many species of ducks, geese, waders and other birdlife populating the old medieval town and port of Francheville. If you're lucky, you may spot a red squirrel, particularly in the woodlands around Newtown. This is the UK's native squirrel and the Isle of Wight is one of only a very few locations where they thrive today, free of the threat posed by the North American 'greys' which have decimated their numbers elsewhere. Unlike their less colourful cousins, the 'reds' are shy, so you'll need to remain quiet.

All of the routes have been tested and then tested again (thanks are extended to Joan, Mary, Matt and Sarah in this regard). The directions and maps provided were accurate at the time of walking (2003-2004). However, this being the Isle of Wight, coastal erosion does have a habit of enforcing footpath deviations from time to time. When this occurs, the Isle of Wight Council, which looks after the path network, is usually swift to define the new route at the point of its departure from the old. Some of the walks feature optional short cuts and/or short detours to places of special interest.

The weather is, of course, a constant factor. After heavy rain, some of the footpath routes can be muddy, waterlogged or even – though it's quite rare – impossible to use. Areas particularly prone to this sort of problem are identified in the walk directions. It's usually advisable to carry rainwear and, when cold, additional layers of clothing, just in case. For the majority of the 15 routes, walking boots or, at least, strong shoes are recommended at all seasons of the year, though this obviously doesn't apply for those few walks confined to town centres or using tarmac pathways throughout.

Train and bus information was correct at the time of writing. Check timetables for changes and service details.

Footpaths on the Isle of Wight are prefixed by initials denoting the parishes through which they run, as follows – A: Arreton, B: Brading, BB: Bembridge, BS: Brighstone, C: Chale, CB: Calbourne,

CS: Cowes, F: Freshwater, G: Gatcombe, GL: Godshill, N: Newport, NC: Newchurch, NT: Niton & Whitwell, R: Ryde, S: Shalfleet, SS: Sandown & Shanklin, SW: Shorwell, V: Ventnor, Y: Yarmouth. If you encounter any obstacles (broken stiles etc) on the country paths, please let the Council's Rights of Way Section know on (01983) 823741.

Great pride is taken by the Island in its footpath network – and in its countryside generally. Please take due regard of notices on stiles and gates which set out specific requests and warn of potential hazards (in truth, there aren't very many). Above all, stay well clear of the cliff edges, especially when walking the high downs in windy conditions, and always follow the Country Code -

- Enjoy the countryside and respect its life and work.
- Guard against all risk of fire.
- Fasten all gates.
- Keep your dogs under close control.
- Keep to public paths across farmland.
- Use gates and stiles to cross fences, hedges and walls.
- Leave livestock, crops and machinery alone.
- Take your litter home.
- Help to keep all water clean.
- Protect wildlife, plants and trees.
- Take special care on country roads.
- Make no unnecessary noise.

The Pine Raft - fossilised
reminder of a primeval forest

Though it transports you back in time all the way to deepest pre-history, this is a short walk of around 2.5 miles (4km) in what Islanders know as the Back of the Wight. It begins with spectacular cliff-top walking along a particularly scenic section of the Isle of Wight Coastal Path above Brook Bay, followed by a countryside ramble just inland. There is no appreciable climbing involved and no stiles (unless the short detour to the old lifeboat station is taken near the end) or difficult obstacles. A limited amount of roadside walking – along the grass verges either side of the coastal Military Road – is necessary, but the route is mostly over well-defined footpaths

Introduction: The village of Brook lies sleepily on the Wealden Beds, the oldest rocks of the Cretaceous series. They were formed in the freshwater lakes and estuaries of the dinosaur's domain, when the forest that lies today at the foot of Hanover Point flourished as a Caribbean-style mix of cycads, zamias, horsetails, palms, giant cacti and, towering above them all, huge dominating conifers. The trees thrived together in lush, humid conditions on what was part of the super-continent modern mankind has retrospectively named Laurasia. And then, 65 million years ago – cataclysm.

Whatever the nature of the global disaster that so dramatically wiped out the dinosaurs, the climatic changes that followed also pronounced the death sentence on the primeval forest. Unable to withstand the much cooler temperature, the trees fell and were washed from a distance along the course of a river until becoming submerged, log-jammed, in the sand at the mouth of the river delta. And there the trunks and branches have lain ever since, long ago turned to stone. The Isle of Wight's Petrified Forest – the Pine Raft – is truly the wreckage of prehistory.

Parking and Public Transport: The walk starts and finishes at Brook Chine's car park, south of the A3055 Military Road, which runs along the Back of the Wight, connecting the south of the Island with its western peninsular. The car park is situated just west of the road junction at Brook Green. Southern Vectis buses on Island Explorer services 7 and 7A (Ryde-Newport-West Wight-Ventnor-Ryde) and 7B (via the more rural Ryde-Newport-West Wight route) stop near the road junction. The 7B has only a restricted service on Sundays, operating between Newport and West Wight only. Brook Chine is also on the circular route of the newly-introduced (2004) West Wight Tour (service 15) from Yarmouth, which operates only at peak periods between April and September.

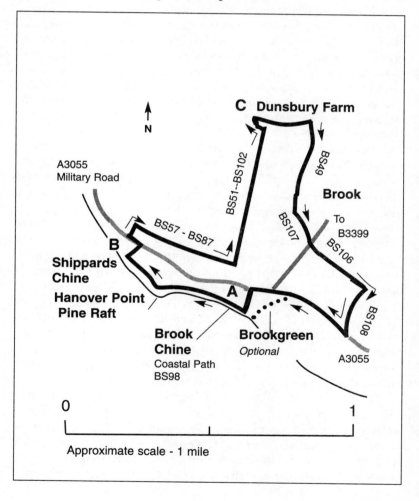

Information: The walk is set in the rural south-west of the Island, some distance from the nearest refreshment outlets – though you may be lucky to find a travelling ice cream van in the summer months. The only toilets *en route* are by the entrance to the car park at Hanover Point.

Directions:
Join the Coastal Path via the gate on the seaward side of Brook Chine car park (grid ref SZ 386835 – marked A on the route map) and turn right (west). Keep to the trodden path, well away from the cliff edge. Hanover Point is clearly visible ahead. After crossing a stream on a wood-planked bridge, climb to a wooden swing gate. Tide and weather permitting, the fossilised remains of the primeval forest are easily distinguishable below the headland and superb views open up along the Back of the Wight, the Island's spectacular south-western coast. *Carry on to pass through a metal gate and follow the well-defined route beyond it to reach the car park for Shippards Chine and Hanover Point ((B on the map – public toilets).*

The fossil forest lies at the heart of the Island's 'dinosaur country' which has yielded some of the UK's finest prehistoric remains. When the tide is low, the footprints of a three-toed dinosaur are revealed in the clay at Brook Bay. The fossilised skeleton of an iguanodon created excitement when it was found at Hanover Point in 1972. More recently, noted finds have included Europe's most complete example of the brachiosaurus. It was discovered in 1992 a short distance south-east of here at Atherfield, an event which led to the setting-up a year later of the Dinosaur Farm Museum, the first of its kind on the Isle of Wight and headquarters for the BBC's *Live from Dinosaur Island* programme in 2002. The programme was well-named. The evidence of dinosaur domination is so abundant and accessible in these parts that the museum organises fossil hunts throughout the year. Its proximity to Brook, just a few miles down the Military Road, makes it an appropriate add-on to the walk.

Go though the car park to its entrance, then, with care, cross the Military Road and go left. After 50 yards (45m), turn right to take footpath F57 (signposted to Brook and The Downs), initially a winding, gravel-surfaced track. Ignore a path going off to the left as the track takes you past Compton Grange (right), smallest of the many outlying farms (granaries) owned by the powerful medieval abbey at Quarr, near present-day Ryde (see walk 6). *The path changes its identity to BS87 (confirmed by the signpost). Now on grass, it runs to a large metal gate and then rises and bends right to reach a second gate. Beyond this, running parallel to the coast, it is soon bordered by hedges as it descends.*

Carry on straight ahead, passing a path junction (marked by a stile on the right), as the route, still running between hedges, rises to another junction and converts to a tarmac-surfaced track alongside houses (Dunsbury Cottages). Go left here, now following footpath BS51 to Dunsbury Farm. The grass path runs straight ahead, then dips to pass through a field. Carry on across a track at an isolated cottage and maintain your direction ahead, staying with the route of BS51, now a surfaced track itself, passing another cottage (right), then further homes (left) to arrive at Dunsbury Farm (C).

Go left, then right with the track through the farmyard. Turn right again, following the signposted route of byway BS86. Ignore the turn-off left, signposted to Brook Down, and walk straight ahead past the farm cottages (right) and uphill to reach the junction with bridleway BS49, signposted to Badger Lane, Brook. Take this path, walking between a hedge and small trees (left) and a fenced-off field. The woodland to the left becomes more substantial further down the path before it reaches a seat at the junction (right) with path BS52. Ignoring the turn-off, continue in the same direction as before, now on path BS107, signposted to Brook village, a section that can be muddy after rain.

The path bears left and narrows to run through an avenue of small trees before dipping, widening again and meeting a farm track trailing in from the left. Carry on ahead, now on a tarmac surface, to pass attractive stone cottages (right), from where the track assumes proper roadway status and arrives at crossroads in Brook.

With care, go straight across and carry on along the route of BS106 (signposted here to Sheep Lane and Military Road), which quickly bears right, downhill. The winding route of the path – now a bridleway – takes you via a metal gate and a section hedge-lined to the left – and often muddy in winter – before rising to a path junction. Turn right here, still following the route of BS106 alongside trees (left), to reach a metal gate and, just beyond, the A3055 roadside. Turn right and walk along the grass verge.

It was the need in the latter half of the 19th century to provide speedier access to the forts in the West Wight – especially at times of perceived threat – that led to the construction of the Military Road between Chale, near the Island's southern tip, and Freshwater Bay, in the west. The road opened up communication along the Back of the Wight which had hitherto been connected to the remainder of the Island solely by cart tracks, running down to it at right-angles to the coast. The realignment that followed at the Freshwater end in 1933 – providing much-needed work for unemployed Welsh miners during the Depression – presented the Isle of Wight with its most dramatically scenic route, though its nearness to the erosion-threatened coast continues to threaten its existence.

After the road bends left, a short detour can be made by crossing to the other side and taking a signposted footpath from Brook towards the coast at Brookgreen. This takes you to the still intact, and identifiable, former Brook lifeboat house. Along with the nearby coastguard cottages, it's a reminder that the trees of the primeval forest are not alone in providing testimony to wreckage in Brook Bay. The need for lifeboat protection along the Island's notorious south-western coast was tragically underlined in the awful winter months towards the end of 1859. In separate incidents on a single day – 5 December – a ferocious south-westerly gale ripped the life from the barque *Mirabita,* smashed to pieces on Brighstone Ledge, and the schooner *Sentinel,* wrecked near Brook. Many lives were lost despite the gallant rescue attempts of local men. But good was to emerge from the tragedy. By the summer of 1860, sufficient money had been raised to equip both Brighstone and Brook with rowing lifeboats, launched simultaneously and manned by local volunteers. The Brook crew and their successors saved 363 lives over the next 76 years before the local station fell victim to the advent of the motorised lifeboats, stationed at Yarmouth and Bembridge, in 1936.

Returning to the Military Road either by the same route or the nearby lane, turn left and use the grass verge to walk the short distance back to the bus stops or the car park where you started the walk.

WALK 2

The Long Stone –
mystical relic of Neolithic man

Set in the rural south-west of the Isle of Wight, this short walk of 2 miles (3.2km) starts with a fairly modest climb up Mottistone Down via the ancient, mystical Long Stone, then descends the down and encircles Mottistone village to the south. The route follows well-defined (though not always signposted) footpaths and bridleways throughout. Stiles are encountered on the descent of the down and the walk involves crossing the B3399 road. Other than that, there are no obstacles.

Introduction: Mottistone is tiny – but hugely significant from an historical perspective as the only location on the Isle of Wight possessing a relic of Neolithic man. The survival of the Long Stone across 5,000 or more years makes it easily the Island's oldest man-made monument. Precisely what its original purpose was is impossible to say with any certainty, but the theory most commonly put forward is that the Long Stone (along with another – possibly its now recumbent companion) was carefully positioned to focus the light of the rising sun into an adjacent long barrow where the ancestors of those who built it lay buried, and where the warmth of the sun's rays would awaken their spirits. Presumably, this occurred only rarely – dawn on midwinter's day is suggested as most likely.

Centuries later, did Saxon elders, as the Long Stone theorists usually maintain, call their men to solemn assembly at the revered site? It became their Moot (or Meeting) Stone, runs the persuasive argument, and this neatly explains the place-name origins of Mottistone, the village which lays below it.

Parking and Public Transport: Parking is available near the start of the walk at the National Trust car park, off the B3399 (Shorwell-Freshwater) road, immediately west of Mottistone Manor, church and village. The start point is a short walk from the bus stops outside the manor house. Buses on Southern Vectis service 7B (Ryde-Newport-Totland) run through Mottistone, though the service is restricted on Sundays to the Newport-Totland section.

Mottistone is also on the circular route of the West Wight Tour (service 15) from Yarmouth, which operates only at peak periods between April and September.

Information: The walk starts and finishes in one of the smallest and quietest Isle of Wight villages and is wholly rural throughout. Toilet and refreshment facilities are non-existent. Seating is provided on Mottistone Down.

Directions:
Begin the walk on the sloping track running from the National Trust car park at its eastern (village) end, across the road from Mottistone Church (grid ref SZ402837). Midway along the track (marked A on the route map – on the left as you leave the car park; on the right if approaching from the bus stops), take the signposted

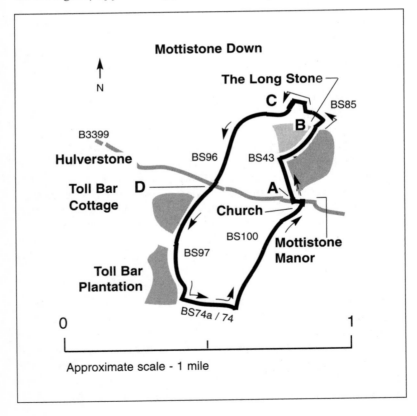

footpath to the Long Stone and the Downs, part of the National Trust-managed Mottistone Estate. The attractive tree-lined path climbs in a cutting (one of the Island's ancient hollow-ways) and eventually reaches a fork in the route soon after passing beneath twisted tree boughs. Follow the rising path to the right. Its course takes you round a sharp right-hand bend to meander through the edge of woodland before rising steeply – a climb assisted by stepping stones – to a wooden gate. Emerging onto a wide track, go straight across and climb the footpath opposite (which can be muddy after rain) to emerge alongside the Long Stone (left – B on the map), set in a clearing at the top.

Sometimes spelt as a single word, sometimes with a hyphen, the Long Stone stands tall, upright, ancient and mysterious, dominating

The Long Stone – the Isle of Wight's only surviving relic of Neolithic man, who probably erected it to focus the light of the rising sun on an adjacent long barrow. Saxons later used it as their 'moot' (or meet) stone, providing the nearby village of Mottistone with its name.

its smaller, horizontal companion. It is fascinating – eerily so on a mist-shrouded day – to stand here and contemplate that the great stone was probably placed here as a device (or part of one) to help refresh the spirits of the buried dead, and to wonder at what explanation for its presence and meaning occurred to the awe-struck Saxons who gathered here thousands of years later.

From the Long Stone, walk a few paces to join the adjacent track and go left, passing Longstone Cottage (right) as you follow its gently rising route to a sharp left-hand turn. Ignoring the gated access to another path on the right, stay on the track as it rounds the bend and, after a short distance, bears sharp right, offering – on a clear day – spectacular coastal views along the Back of the Wight. Carry on along the track, eventually passing a seat (left) and rounding a left-hand bend so that you are now heading in the direction of the coast. A short distance further on, turn left off the track to follow the route of a well-defined, but un-signed, footpath descending between banks into a cutting (C).

Bordered initially by small trees, the winding path eventually 'opens up' on the right to reveal another view of the south-western coastal belt before threading its way through high gorse, then passing to the right of a tall bank and continuing through a shallow cutting to arrive at a track. Bearing slightly to the right, cross the track to pass through a wooden swing gate and resume the descent – initially via a much steeper section – of Mottistone Down with the aid of rough-cut steps. The path's winding route downwards becomes less steep as it runs alongside small trees to reach a stile.

Beyond the stile, the path adopts a route between a small bank (left) and a fenced-off field (coastal views) before skirting round more gorse bushes – resplendent with yellow blossom in spring – and terminating, via a stile, at the side of the B3399, opposite Toll Bar Cottage (D). Cross the road with care, bearing slightly right, to use another stile providing access to footpath BS97 (signposted to Military Road). The sloping path, bordered initially by hedgerows, crosses a small stream and continues between trees (left) and a field boundary fence to wind through Toll Bar Plantation. Well-defined, its route eventually emerges at the edge of the wood to run alongside a field (left) and cross a stream on a double-planked bridge. Passing to the side of a second field, the path crosses another stream to arrive at an undesignated pathway 'T' junction. Go left here.

Running between hedgerows, the wide grass path soon passes an opening on the left – junction for a bridleway (also undesignated) – and continues until forming a 'T' junction with a rough-surfaced track. Turn left and follow the track's dead straight, rising route between hedges all the way back to Mottistone village. Immediately before the village, the track becomes a surfaced roadway and bends right (away from its junction with signposted footpath BS74) to pass cottages, with the spire of Mottistone's St Peter & St Paul's Church clearly visible ahead.

Perched on a modest mound, the church has 12th century origins, though they're hard to find nowadays following extensive rebuilding by the illustrious Island families – Chekes, Dillingtons and Seelys – who have lived in turn at the nearby manor house, An interesting feature is the chancel roof, constructed of cedar from the stricken barque *Cedarine,* salvaged by the Brighstone lifeboat crew – their first-ever call-out – in April 1862. The vessel's misfortune, battered by a heavy groundswell after being caught on Brighstone Ledge in thick fog, added further punishment for the majority of her 234-strong human cargo – 191 were convicts returning from Bermuda after serving their time in the colony. Eight trips by the lifeboat brought 134 people safely ashore, including women, children and crew members.

Ignoring the left turn immediately before the church, carry on ahead down this quiet road (Church Lane) to emerge again at the side of the B3399, a few feet from the bus stops on either side.

As noted, the manor of Mottistone boasts an impressive pedigree of ownership. There was a Saxon manor house on the site of the present building before the manor itself fell into the hands of the powerful Norman family of de Insula – the name reflected their adopted Island home and was later changed to Lisle. The present house was built centuries later by the Cheke dynasty, with the earliest part – the east wing – dating back to the 15th century. Robert Dillington, who already lived in the splendid accommodation provided at Knighton Gorges, in the east of the Island, added Mottistone to his impressive collection of Isle of Wight manors in the 17th century.

A prolonged period of decline – when the house was tenanted and served merely as a farmhouse – came to an end in 1861 with its purchase, as part of the Mottistone Estate, by the Nottinghamshire coalowner Charles Seely, whose wealth had already provided him with a comfortable retirement at nearby Brook House, where he continued to live until his death in 1887. His son, also named

Charles, is remembered chiefly on the Island for his role in setting up the library service, a model for others elsewhere in the country, while Charles's son, General Jack Seeley, is recalled for all sorts of reasons – courageous soldier, Cabinet Minister, Lord Lieutenant for more than 30 years and legendary lifeboatman (and eventually coxswain) with the Brook crew whenever his many other commitments allowed.

It was General Jack who finally took the Seely family into residence at Mottistone Manor. His restoration of the east wing – partially buried since a catastrophic landslide early in the 18th century – proved the first step in a total restoration of the old house, completed under the supervision of the General's architect son, John. When John Seeley died in 1963, the Mottistone estate was bequeathed to the National Trust. It wasn't the end of the Seely family's links with the manor. General Jack's stepson, Sir John Nicholson, a recent Lord Lieutenant of the Island himself, lives there today.

Cross the road and turn left to arrive back at the National Trust car park.

A Bronze Age Mound –
by way of a Space Age test site

This spectacular walk of around 6 miles (9.6km) in the far west of the Island threads through a rich tapestry of local history right up to the Space Age *en route* to an outstanding reminder of Bronze Age burial on Headon Warren. It takes you to the best viewpoint of The Needles and passes close to the famous coloured sands at Alum Bay. Apart from the climb up to the burial mound, towards the end of the walk, the hard work is on the outward leg. The initial climb from Totland to the summit of Tennyson Down is gradual to begin with, but steeper over its final sections. There are only a few stiles, the route is easy to follow and roadside walking is confined to the usually quiet streets around Totland. This walk is a real treat – but remember to stay clear of the cliff edges.

Introduction: Bronze Age burial sites are not hard to find on the Isle of Wight. Inevitably, many have been ploughed over and otherwise eroded so that the distinctive round barrow is all but obliterated – indeed, *completely* obliterated in some cases, identifiable only to those who can interpret the distinguishing marks on the ground that betray the existence of a former mound. Others survive sufficiently intact to serve as fascinating features of country walks over a wide area of the Island. In that sense, the burial mound on Headon Warren at Totland is one of many. However, there is a difference.

It's one of only a few surviving from the *early* part of the Bronze Age and is unusual in having its identity and purpose drawn to the attention of the many walkers who tramp this section of the Island's Coastal Path. This is partly the reason for selecting the Headon mound to illustrate the Bronze Age period (roughly, the one thousand years from 1,700 BC). It is also chosen because its position near the western tip of the Island places it within an extraordinary cross-section of Isle of Wight history and – geographically at least – sets the Bronze Age virtually side by side with the Space Age.

Parking and Public Transport: Totland is the furthest west village on the Isle of Wight, accessible via Yarmouth or Freshwater from the principal roads running to the West Wight from the remainder of the Island. Free car parking is available off The Broadway, Totland's main street, a short distance before the start point of the walk at the war memorial. Buses on Southern Vectis Island Explorer routes 7, 7A and 7B (Ryde-Newport-West Wight) serve the village, although the 7B is restricted to the Newport-Totland section on Sundays. The Sundays-excepted service 11 (Newport-Totand) is a further possibility, as is the local Wight Bus service 13 (Freshwater-Totland circular). To add a bit of fun to the bus journey, Totland is also on the route of Southern Vectis open-top service 47, which operates between Yarmouth bus station and The Needles. The main Totland bus stops are on The Broadway, a few paces from the memorial.

Information: Totland has the full range of village facilities, including a pub and other refreshment outlets. Refreshment stops may also be taken *en route* at the isolated High Down Inn, in The Needles Pleasure Park and at Totland Pier. Toilets are available at or near all these locations. At its midway point, the route also provides immediate access to Old Needles Battery, open to the public.

Directions:
Beginning the walk at Totland's war memorial (grid ref SZ322871 – marked A on the route map), with your back to the village centre, go left along Weston Road (by the garage), soon passing some of the village's older thatched homes. Climb this pleasant road beyond Totland Community Primary School (right) before turning left at a 'T' junction into Hurst Hill. Still climbing, turn right after a short distance to follow Weston Lane's winding, undulating and increasingly rural route past the striking modernity of St Saviour's Roman Catholic Church (left) and, by way of contrast, some interesting domestic architecture (right) before the lane bends left and climbs to crossroads immediately before the High Down Inn. Exercising care when crossing the junction, carry on in the same direction, past the pub, now following Highdown Lane as it dips and then climbs steeply to its termination in an old quarry below the final section of the climb to the summit of Tennyson Down.
Look for a well-trodden path going off to the left and follow

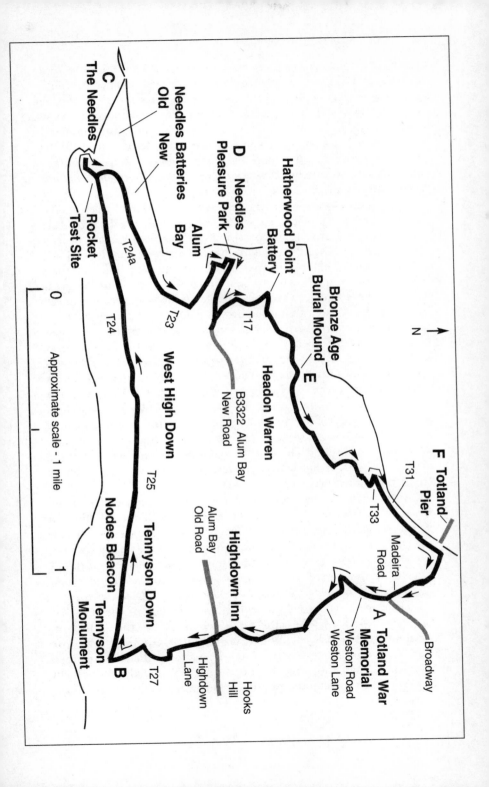

this as, after a short distance, it rises onto an area of grass, with a seat (right). Go sharp right, using the well-defined stepped footpath as it winds and climbs, via a wooden swing gate, towards the summit. It's worth taking a breather midway to admire the view (right) of Totland and, beyond it, the Western Solent and mainland shore: indeed, the village's name is probably derived from Tout-land (look-out land). *The path eventually emerges between bushes onto grass just below the Tennyson Monument. Complete the climb to the monument (B on the map).*

Tennyson Down (the name at least) is, of course, allied to the Golden Age of the Victorian poets, rather than the Bronze Age. When Alfred Lord Tennyson lived at Farringford, in nearby Freshwater (he moved there with his devoted wife, Emily, in 1853 and it remained their principal home for the remainder of their lives), the hill was known as High Down. How much of the great works the Poet Laureate produced while on the Island were inspired by his fondness for walking the downs is fascinating conjecture.

The origins for perhaps the simplest, and arguably the most moving, of all his poems can be linked firmly to the Island, or at least to the ferry trip from Lymington. *Crossing the Bar* was conceived on a railway steamer in 1889, when the poet was in his 81st year. He wrote it as a hymn of thanksgiving for his recent recovery from serious illness, but the words betray an awareness that his life was ebbing away. Tennyson's earthly destination may have been the Island's western ferry berth at Yarmouth, but it was, of course, a metaphor. The 'bar' he was soon to cross would – if the hope expressed in his words converted to reality – lead him to "meet my maker, face to face" in Heaven.

Turn right at the monument to walk along the narrowing promontory towards the Island's western extremity. Follow a central, straight line, well away from the cliff edge on the left – especially in windy conditions – as you soak up the heady cocktail of spectacular coastal scenery and fresh air (weather permitting!). *After a distance, look out for what appears to be an old signal beacon, rising above gorse bushes to the right. Walk towards it.*

The beacon is actually a scaled-down replica of the one that formerly stood on the site now occupied by the Tennyson Monument. The Isle of Wight was rightly proud of its close association with the great poet. High Down was officially re-named Tennyson Down following his death in 1892 and the monument was erected to 'crown' the summit in his memory. The stump of the old signal beacon that made way for it – one of the many beacons across the Island that would have been lit to warn of impending invasion – was uprooted and subsequently moved to its present site, alongside the replica. *Carry on in the same direction, over a stile, following the signposted route of the Coastal Path to The Needles between the gorse. The path is usually well-defined as it rises onto open grassland. In the distance, former coastguard cottages (to the right) provide an early sight of the buildings on the headland at the Island's western tip. Your route takes you leftwards, heading towards a solitary signal mast, with views of Alum Bay to the right. Carry on to reach a stile, immediately before the mast, then walk to the left of its compound and follow a chalk path descending to a concrete roadway (left).*

It's an incongruous sight. Not the most obvious location for a promenade, though it does overlook a natural amphitheatre, stretching as far as the cliff edge. In fact, the roadway and the truncated remains of the chambered structures attached to it are relics of Britain's early involvement in the Space Age. An information board across the road provides the full history of this extraordinary site. Briefly, it was constructed to test-fire the engines manufactured by Saunders-Roe at East Cowes between 1956 and 1971 for the Black Knight and Black Arrow rocket projects. Nothing actually took off from here. The rockets themselves were later tested in Woomera, Australia, before the UK's stuttering space programme itself was grounded, leaving the road to nowhere at The Needles.

Cross to the other side to take a short signposted path leading, via a series of steps, to the best viewpoint of The Needles rocks themselves (C on the map). The three huge chalk stacks, stepping stones for giants out to the famous granite lighthouse, bear little resemblance to anything you would choose to sew with. The one that did – the original Needle rock- crumbled into a storm-lashed sea as long ago as 1764. The gap it left is obvious, but the larger gap is beyond the lighthouse – across the sea to the effective continuation of The Needles at Old Harry Rocks, off the Dorset coast at Swanage. The Solent's breach of the hard chalk which acted as Wight's umbilical cord with mainland England happened around 5,000 BC, many thousands of years after the melting of the Ice Age.

Retrace your steps back to the concrete roadway, then go left along it to climb past the coastguard look-out (left) and follow the road as it bends sharp right into the remains of the New Needles Battery.

This early 19th century engraving of The Needles from Scratchells Bay closely matches the view from the walk route – though at shore, rather than cliff-top, level.

The coast either side of the The Needles Passage, the western entrance to The Solent, was first equipped with defensive fortifications centuries before the Victorians, fearful to the point of panic of French invasion (see walk 11) constructed the batteries here on the Island's western promontory. Right out on the point, Old Needles Battery stands some 250 feet (76m) above the sea. It was built between 1861 and 1863, with Alum Bay as part of its defensive responsibilities, and was surrounded by a dry ditch just in case the French evaded its guns and swarmed up to it from the beach.

The battery remained as part of the nation's coastal defences for the best part of a century via successive changes in specific military use and modernisations that culminated with the installation of radar during the Second World War. 'Mothballing' followed in 1945, the radar went in 1950 and the adjacent fire command post, which had once directed all the guns guarding the sea passage, was abolished in 1953. Twenty-two years later, ownership of the site passed to the National Trust, as part of its acquisition of the entire headland, and in 1982, restored, it was opened to the public by the Prince of Wales. A visit is recommended. The access walkway is clearly signposted.

New Needles Battery followed in 1893-95. The arrival of larger barrels for the guns created a stir in 1914. Landed at Colwell Bay, they were effectively dragged by horses through the streets westwards and then up to the battery via the access road from Alum Bay, which had been laid out in 1899. Though not continuously manned thereafter, the battery was called into action in a 'counter bombardment' role during the Second World War, ready to repel enemy attempts to block the sea channel. In the event, it was troubled more by the Luftwaffe in the sky above. Radar was also installed here, but 'mothballing' followed in 1945 and the guns were scrapped two years later.

Some of the battery's structures on the southern side were adapted for use in the rocket engine tests, but most of the military buildings were demolished after the National Trust acquired the headland. Those bits that remain are identified and explained by information panels.

With your back to the battery emplacements, go left, down the tarmac access roadway for a short distance until it bends sharp left. Leave the road here to take the signposted Coastal Path route (right) along, and then down, a well-defined chalk path to reach a stile. Go down the steps beyond it and rejoin the access road for the remainder of the descent (right) to The Needles Pleasure Park above Alum Bay. Use of the road by motor traffic is limited, but watch out for the open-top bus operating its shuttle service from and to Yarmouth if you elect to walk on the tarmac rather than the path which, for most of the way down, runs alongside it on the left-hand side. Take note of the signs warning against straying too close to the cliff edge.

The many different beds of sand that form the cliffs of Alum Bay in a dazzling complexity of colour are seen to good advantage on the descent from the headland. There's not as much as there used to be, though. Many a shelf and mantlepiece the world over is adorned by multi-hued examples of the famous sands. artistically arranged in small, decorative glass containers. You used to be able to help yourself to it, but the dangerous instability of the cliffs put a stop to that some years ago.

Fine white sand from the bay was extensively used in the production of glass throughout the 18th and 19th centuries, The business has been revived in recent years – glass-making is now among the attractions at The Needles Pleasure Park, which also provides access to the only chair lift on the Island. It takes you down to the shore at the foot of the cliffs and boats offering short excursions out to The Needles – but not from Alum Bay Pier (built 1887), of which no trace now remains.

Stay with the road as, eventually, it bends left to enter the extensive grounds of the pleasure park (passing a garden on the left locally famous as the gnome capital of the Isle of Wight!). *Inside the park (D on the map), bear right to take the sloping route between the parking areas towards the glass factory/shop and the public toilets just beyond it. Cross the road to the left-hand side and bear right, out of the park and along the pavement, still following the signposted route of the Coastal Path. After a short distance, it takes you sharp left, away from the road, onto the access route to the Headon Hall Estate and, further on, through barriers (right) to a country path climbing onto Headon Warren, signposted as part of the Coastal Path.*

Climb with the path as it bends right, then left between hedges – offering another view of The Needles, behind you to the left. The route passes a panel giving information on the warren's environment, then rises to bear right to reach a pathway 'T' junction. Go left here onto a flat area of grass, near the remains of the former Hatherwood Point Battery. Built in the 1860s to help defend Alum Bay and the shipping channel in the Western Solent, the site was subject to soil erosion from an early stage. Its last military function was as a Royal Navy indicator loop station during the Second World War. Since then, the eroding coastline – aided by demolition – has left only crumbling granite and concrete amid the vegetation (just beyond the flat ground) as a reminder of former importance.

Bear right, away from the grassed area, to follow a chalk path as it climbs to the top of the warren, providing a good view (right) of the outward leg of the walk on West High Down. Further remains of military installations – Headon Warren was once a fire command station for all the batteries in the area – are visible near the summit of the climb. *Carry on along the path, passing a seat (right), as it twists and turns, but generally follows a route straight ahead, to reach a barrier* – and bring this multi-layered walk through Isle of Wight history to its Bronze Age objective (E).

As noted, the burial mound protected by the barrier is from the early Bronze Age and is one of only a few from that period remaining in the Island. The information panel tells of the probable origins of the mound (and two smaller examples in the field below) around 1,500 BC. They were constructed above the graves of departed leaders. The Isle of Wight has yielded important archaeological finds from this period. The British Museum holds probably the most spectacular – the spearheads, flanged axes, daggers and other metalwork collectively known as the Arreton Down hoard.

Down the centuries, excavation and plunder by treasure-hunters, together with the erosion caused by the feet of countless walkers tramping over the top, have seriously damaged the integrity of the mound on Headon Warren. Its decline has been halted by stressing the importance of the site and deterring present-day walkers from going straight over it. *Instead, go left, around the mound, then follow the well-trodden path ahead.* The view along the coast (left) includes the pier at Totland Bay, penultimate destination on the walk route.

The path eventually bends sharply to the left and winds around the side of a field, descending between hedges, then turns sharp right and runs down onto a track providing access to Warren Cottage. Go left, down the track, to emerge at the roadside, where the directional sign (pointing back) confirms that you have been using footpath T17 through the warren. Cross the road and go left, downhill, passing the attractive houses on this quiet approach to Totland. Ignoring footpaths T16 (signposted to Alum Bay, left) and T14 (right), stay with the road as it bends right, then left. At the next right-hand bend, turn left to take footpath T33, signposted to Widdick Chine and Beach.

The path descends quite steeply before veering left to the start of steps, which take you right down to the seawall at Widdick Chine. Go right here, past Totland's old lifeboat house (1885-1924), and continue the waterfront walk all the way to Totland Pier (F – passing public toilets just before reaching it). Once regularly visited by railway steamers from the mainland, the Victorian pier is a rare survivor that has benefited from recent restoration work, though much remains to be done.

With your back to the pier entrance/café, use the steps in front of you to climb away from the shore, turning right at the top to follow the path to the roadside. Cross the road (left) to join Madeira Road, which leads you back to The Broadway and the finish of the walk.

Encircling the haven-side villa of Roman Vectis

Brading's Roman villa is the outstanding relic on the Isle of Wight of the Emperor Claudius's 1st century conquest of Britain. This walk of just over 3.5 miles (5.6km) encircles the villa that once sat in splendid isolation above the waters of Brading Haven. Very much a 'walk of two halves' – the outward leg climbs to the summit of the local downland; the return leg brings you back down again – it is testing in places, but follows a well-defined route for most of its length. There are a number of stiles to negotiate and some roadside walking, though for the most part on quiet country lanes.

Introduction: Britons fought bravely to hold up the Roman occupation of their homeland until the modern, well-disciplined forces of the super-power finally proved too much for the half-naked, barely trained and poorly-armed Celtic defenders. That, at least, was the general situation. It seems unlikely that it happened quite like that on the Isle of Wight. When the 2nd Legion, led by Vespasian, took the island "near Britain" (the words of his biographer Suetonius), it is doubtful whether a resident population numbering a few hundred at most would, or could, have offered much meaningful resistance. Suetonius offers little in the way of clarification. The offshore isle was "brought under our rule" is about as far as he goes in shedding any light on the matter.

Potentially, the 34-year-old future Emperor had thousands of men under his command as he set about annexing substantial parts of the south for the imperial cause. Yet, Roman military artefacts are conspicuous by their total absence among the archaeological evidence from the 1st century occupation of the island the empire would name Vectis. That suggests its conquest in AD 43 was a peaceful one.

Parking and Public Transport: Brading lies on the A3055 between Ryde and Sandown. The main car park is off the High Street (to the left as you enter the town from Ryde). Limited parking is available at the rail station, start point for the walk. The station is served by

Island Line's Ryde-Shanklin trains. The ferry-rail interchange at Ryde Pier Head means the walk can easily be undertaken on a day trip from the mainland. Brading's principal bus services are provided by Southern Vectis on routes 7, 7A and 7B (Ryde-Shanklin-Ventnor-West Wight). The town is also served in summer by the open-top service 44 (Ryde-Sandown), the Tuesdays only service 90 (Sandown-Bembridge-Newport) and the Optio service 104, which runs on demand. (Sandown-Yaverland-Brading), which calls at the rail station. Brading's main bus stops are at the town centre Bull Ring.

Information: Soon after the start, the walk passes through Brading town centre, where a full range of facilities (including three pubs, other refreshment outlets and public toilets) are available. Beyond the town, the route is in open countryside, but refreshment facilities are available *en route* at Adgestone Vineyard's café, when open, and – depending on season and weather – you may also be lucky enough to find one of the ice cream vans which are often parked on Brading Down.

Directions:
Leaving the rail station (grid ref SZ609869 – marked A on the route map), walk up Station Road towards the town centre. The Downs, rising above the town, dominates the view ahead as you pass the junction with Lower Furrlongs (right) and walk for a short distance alongside the main A3055 into the area known as the Bull Ring. As the main road bends right, use the pedestrian crossing to reach the far side and bear right, past the shops, to reach the West Street junction (public toilets – B on the map).

While the pre-reclamation haven (see walk 13) probably supported a scattered community of fisher-people, civilisation came to the area surrounding that vast expanse of inland water with the Romans. There is evidence to suggest that what was to become the villa at Morton, overlooking the haven, originated within the first decade of 1st century Roman occupation as a few simple timber buildings. Some suggest the site was developed as a home-from-home for none other than Vespasian himself during his period of governing the Isle of Wight on behalf of the occupying power – though this may be little more than a tempting historical fantasy.

What is certain is that, by the early part of the 4th century (AD 300 onwards), those early wooden structures had been transformed

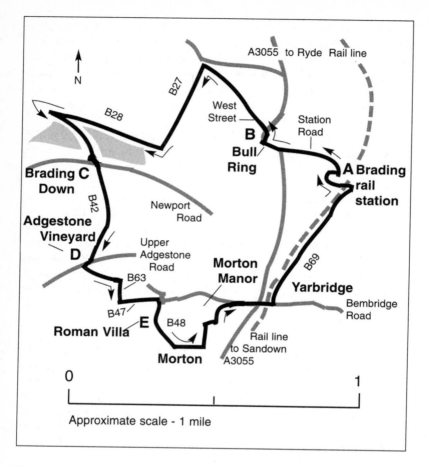

into an extensive and complex farmhouse, its buildings grouped around a courtyard, which was without doubt the residence of someone of considerable importance. It would have been an isolated home and probably remained so until the Romans finally retreated from Britain in AD 410.

The invasion fleets that followed the Romans into the haven in subsequent centuries were considerably more hostile. Most spectacularly – if one interpretation of the *Anglo-Saxon Chronicle* is to be believed – this was the setting for an epic sea battle in AD 897 between the Saxon forces of Alfred the Great and the latest Viking hoardes to threaten the security of the Isle of Wight. There was considerable loss of life as the fighting spread inland from the haven. According to local folklore, the blood of the Danes who fought Alfred's men to the death intermingled with that of the slain Saxons and still runs in the stream through Bloodstone Copse. near the supposed scene of the fighting.

Despite frequent foreign incursions, Brading managed to develop on the bank of the haven, from village to both corporate borough – its first charter was granted by Edward I in 1280 – and seaport. It no longer enjoys the status of either, but the evidence of former importance and prestige is remarkably well preserved. A quick tour of the compact town centre will reveal the old lock-up, whipping post and stocks, The former town pound is preserved close by, all of them in close proximity to the wax museum, occupying what is claimed – though it has rivals – to be the oldest house on the Island still standing. And then there's the bull ring. Many towns and cities have bull rings, but they are mere names, recalling former use in a more cruel age. It's not just a name in Brading. The bull ring itself is still there, prominently displayed in front of the 'new' town hall (look to the right) following its re-location in recent years from the centre of the road.

Bear left along West Street, passing thatched cottages (right) before climbing to, and beyond, a right-hand bend in the road. Passing between posts, follow the rising tarmac path ahead as it threads between open downland (left) and housing. Exercise caution near the far end of the path as it forms a junction with Kyngs Close (right) and adopts the status of a narrow road. *Soon after this, as the route bends right and descends to another junction, turn left to follow the route of public footpath B27, signposted to Brading Down.*

Keeping the hedge to your right, stay with the path as it climbs up the side of a field and a few paces beyond it to reach a stile. Turn right over the stile, skirting a wooded area (left) as you continue the climb along the widening track (path B28), which dips and then rises again before forming a junction with another path trailing in from a higher level on the left, the next part of the route. This path (B29) is not identified by a sign and is easy to miss. (If you should inadvertently go past this junction, you'll arrive a few minutes later at another – this time signposted – where footpath B59 goes off right to Nunwell and Hardingshute. Turn round here and retrace your route back to the missed turning).

Follow the path through the copse as the climb steepens towards a wooden gate. Go through it into the field beyond and

Centuries after the Romans had departed, Brading developed as an important medieval town and inland port. This late-19th century lithograph by Percy Stone depicts both the fine medieval church and the old town hall – still there today, complete with stocks, whipping-post and lock-up!

bear right up a well-trodden path – heading for a line of small trees – to reach a metal gate providing access to the roadside on Brading Down. Cross the road with care into the viewpoint parking area (C on the map) and veer slightly to the left to a small gate marked by a footpath sign to begin the descent of the Down towards the Roman villa.

With views ahead of the coastline along Sandown Bay, *follow the trodden path in the direction indicated by the sign as far as a hedge-lined fence, then go left alongside it and, soon afterwards, right through a gap to reach a wooden gate, where the footpath sign confirms you are on path B42, heading in the direction of Adgestone. Carry on down its pleasant, winding route, bordered by small trees and bushes, as it deepens into a cutting and then skirts the cultivated slopes of Adgestone Vineyard (right) before taking you to the side of Upper Adgestone Road, alongside the entrance to the vineyard and its café. (D).*

Cross this usually quiet road, bearing slightly right to go down the lane opposite, soon arriving at another junction. Carry on ahead, veering slightly left, and climb the short distance to stiles on either side of the road. Go over the right-hand stile to follow the route of path B63 (signposted to Sandown) through a field. Some way into the field, the path is dissected by another (though you will almost certainly encounter more than one apparent contender for the definitive route!). *Go left here and follow the path (B47) until it bears left to exit the field at a point marked by a footpath signpost, where steps (left) descend to the roadside. Turn sharp right here, now following the signposted B48 to the Roman villa at Morton between hedgerow (left) and fencing. The path takes you to the villa's entrance (right – E on the map).*

When the Romans left Britain, the villa at Morton crumbled into ruin. Down the centuries, the remains gradually disappeared below the rising ground and lay forgotten for the best part of the next 1,500 years.

Then, in the spring of 1879, a retired officer of the merchant navy called Captain Thorpe, with a deep interest in Roman antiquities, was strolling near the boundary of Morton Farm when his attention was drawn to two small children playing near a hedge as their father – who farmed the adjacent holding – ploughed his field. The children were arguing. Each of them wanted possession of something that had been turned up by the plough. Intrigued, Captain Thorpe asked them to show him what they found. He at

The first illustration of the excavated Roman villa at Morton. The picture dates from October 1880 – the year after the villa's chance discovery.

once recognised it as a shard of first century Samian pottery.

"Have you ever seen any pieces like this in your field before?' he asked the children's father excitedly.

"Hundred of 'em, drat 'em," answered the farmer, "and stones and great tiles, too."

"What do you do with them when you find them?"

"Do with 'em! Why, I throw 'em into the ditch."

And that, apparently, was the precise bit of dialogue that was to lead to the discovery and excavation – by Sir Henry Oglander – of Brading Roman villa. It was something of an irony that the gradual process of uncovering the villa coincided with the withdrawal of the water from the haven it had been built to overlook. The magnificent mosaics in the preserved west wing are the villa's most exciting feature, but there is a great deal more to see of the Romano-British farming estate – and still more of it awaits excavation in the years to come. The latest development by the Oglander Roman Trust, which manages the site, is the construction of a new protective 'over-building' and visitor centre. The work was still in progress as this book was being prepared for publication (2004) and, initially at least, this may affect the course of public rights of way in the proximity of the villa.

Follow the waymarked route onto the approach road and stay with it until, eventually, it bends left and runs down to its junction with Morton Old Road. Go left here, passing Morton Farmhouse (right) and then, after a right-hand bend, Morton Mews, before the road bends left into Morton Manor Road. The manor house dates from 1249 and was probably built for the descendents of the de Aula family, whose arrival on the Island was a consequence of the Norman Conquest two centuries earlier. Much altered in later centuries, the house is famed for its gardens, a magnificent combination of the formal and informal, and has its own vineyard. Now integrated with Brading, Morton itself began life as a waterside hamlet on the edge of Brading Haven – the placename is Anglo-Saxon for "by the water."

Follow this road as it climbs and bends right to reach another junction. Turn right and walk the short distance down the hill to the main A3055 at Yarbridge. Cross the road with care when the traffic lights allow and continue straight ahead (using the path on the right-hand side) down Bembridge Road, which dips past the Yarbridge pub (right) and then rises to cross the railway line. Immediately beyond the railway bridge, cross the road to go through a wooden gate, marked by a footpath sign, and down steps to the lineside path leading back to Brading station. Just before the station platforms, cross a stile and follow the path (left) across the track – when clear – before turning right, crossing another stile and using the path ahead as it follows a winding route into Station Road, a few yards from the station itself (right).

In the shadow of the Island's impregnable Norman fortress

Set amid the downland immediately south of Carisbrooke, the route of this 6-mile (9.6km) country ramble is mainly on rural footpaths, taking in some of the Island's ancient trackways, but also includes sections along pretty country lanes largely devoid of traffic. Some climbing is involved as the route ascends Dukem Down and, later, rises again as it heads back to Carisbrooke from Gatcombe village. For most of the way the paths are well trodden and easy to follow, though there are a few stiles to negotiate and some sections of the walk can be muddy after rain. The scenery makes the effort worthwhile and, while you are never more than a few miles from Newport's town centre, there is a general feeling of rural tranquility from start to finish.

Introduction: Occupying a commanding, lofty position just west of Newport, capital of the Isle of Wight, the castle of Carisbrooke may well have been a defensive strongfold for Ancient Britons and Romans alike before the Saxons built a fortified camp (known as a 'burgh') here as protection against Viking invasion. However, the still partially-intact castle dominating the skyline today belongs firmly to the Norman era. Its post-Conquest history is synonymous with that of the Isle of Wight itself. A tour of the ruins and remaining structures – including the museum and wellhouse, where the treadwheel is still worked by the castle's famous donkeys – is recommended as an 'add on' to the walk.

Carisbrooke Castle provides the Island's most majestic reminder of Norman architecture, but the period is also recalled at several local churches. The 13th century building at St Olave's, Gatcombe, also on the walk route, is not the oldest among them, but it is definately one of the Island's ecclesiastical gems.

Parking and Public Transport: Car parking is available at Carisbrooke Castle itself, start point for the walk, or off the High Street in the village below. To access the castle, heading west from Newport, leave Carisbrooke Road at the war memorial to bear left along Castle Road and then go up Castle Hill, which can also be reached from Carisbrooke's village centre via Cedar Hill. The Island Explorer bus routes 7, 7A and 7B, operated by Southern Vectis, all serve Carisbrooke from Ryde, Newport and the West Wight, as does the Newport-Totland service 11 and the Newport local service 38.

A pleasant way of extending the walk is to approach the start point on foot from Carisbrooke village by turning left near the top of the High Street into Castle Street, then bearing right, via a picturesque ford, into Millers Lane and using one of two signposted footpath routes (left) up to the castle.

Information: With all but the section at Gatcombe in open countryside, the route's only comfort facility is the village tea room at Little Gatcombe Farm. Signs displayed in Gatcombe Road and outside the farm itself indicate when the tea room is open. A full range of facilities (including pubs, toilets and shops) is available in the village of Carisbrooke and, of course, at nearby Newport.

Directions:
He who holds Carisbrooke holds the Island, runs the old adage. The first to do so following William the Conqueror's triumph at the Battle of Hastings in 1066 was his trusted kinsman, William FitzOsbern. Given the castle by the Conqueror as a token of gratitude for his unwavering support, FitzOsbern soon began the transformation from Saxon 'burgh' to Norman fortress. Strategically important to the nation as a whole – the Island has always been a potential stepping-stone to full-scale invasion of the mother country – Carisbrooke became the seat of Wight government for FitzOsbern and the succession of Norman lords who subsequently held sway here. Initially, the Island was run as a self-contained fiefdom, with allegiance and loyalty sworn to the Lord of the Island rather than to the King.

In 1136, the first significant written reference to the fortress described it as "a stately castle built of hewn stone," though by then it was in the hands of the FitzOsberns' successors, the de Redvers family, who held it for nearly 200 years and were responsible for building much of what can be seen today. The remarkable Countess Isabella de Fortibus, who ruled the Island for an astonishing 30 years and was the last of the de Redvers line, signed the Castle over to the Crown on her deathbed in 1293.

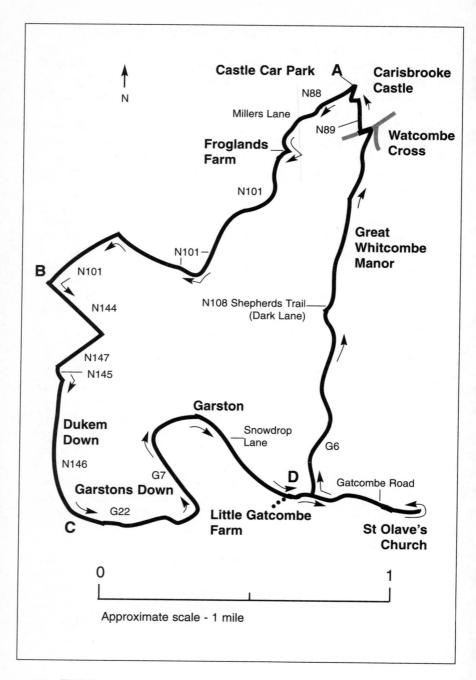

Having sampled some of the early history of the Norman castle, *begin the walk from the section of the car park furthest from the castle (grid ref SZ484877 – marked A on the route map) by taking signposted public footpath N88 to Millers Lane. which descends from the car park's northern boundary. On reaching the lane, which is virtually traffic-free, turn left and follow its route up, then down, to reach a ford. Use the path on its right to proceed. Continue up the winding lane, bearing right at the 'Y' junction ahead and soon passing Froglands Farm,*

Leaving the tarmac roadway, join the rough-surfaced path ahead before bearing right to follow the route of a signposted public bridleway (N101), offering views (right) back to Carisbrooke village. The narrowing path reaches a section which can be muddy and waterlogged in places after heavy rain, *as it climbs, then descends and turns right to pass on the way down footpath junctions left and right (the signposted N104 to Clatterford and Carisbrooke). Stay on the bridleway to the foot of its descent. With a hedge in front of you, and a sloping grass path to the right, take the well-trodden, hedge-lined route to the left.*

With Bowcombe Down to the right of you, continue along this path until it forms a 'T' junction with a trackway (B on the map).

The Castle and village of Carisbrooke – an early-19th century view.

Go left here, following the route of the Old Highway (path N144) to Gatcombe. Passing another footpath joining it on the left, stay on the N144 as it enters an area of open landscape, then bear sharp right at a waymark post. At the next waymark, a short distance further on, turn left up a climbing path to reach a wooden gate (right). Go through the gate and continue to climb, skirting a copse (right), to pass through a second gate. Carry on straight ahead, over a stile, to follow for some distance the line of fencing to your left as you near the top of Dukem Down.

The path eventually bends left, takes you through another wooden gate, and then a metal gate, before running to the left of a conifer plantation. Stay on the path until reaching its junction with path G22 (to Gatcombe) on your left (C on the map). Take this path through a gate and then downhill, keeping the fence to your left as you descend amid the glorious downland scenery. Some way down, look out for a metal gate (left) where the directional sign indicates the path's' continuation towards Garston. Follow it as it winds down the side of the hill (Garston Down), eventually running alongside a fence (right) and bearing left to pass through a waymarked metal gate. A footpath directional sign (pointing in the opposite direction) indicates that the path is now designated G7.

Carry on to pass through a second gate and eventually reach a waymark post. Turn right here and walk to the foot of the hill, veering right to emerge at Garston via a gate into a small farmyard and continuing past cottages into a lane. Turn right when the lane runs into another, ignoring the bridleway ahead, and take this most rural of roads (Snowdrop Lane) down its attractive route until, after passing the stone-built Snowdrop Cottage (right), it forms a junction with Newbarn Lane, on the edge of Gatcombe village (D).

The route takes you left at this point but you may wish to make a very short detour to the right as far as Little Gatcombe Farm and its welcoming tea room. Walkers with muddy boots should note that 'disposable footies' are provided here, so there's no excuse for making a mess of the tea room floor! Check the signs outside, but it's open all year round, normally between 12noon and 5.30pm.

Back on the route, bear left from Snowdrop Lane and enjoy the stone, thatch and sheer tranquility of this delightfully secluded and unspoilt village to reach St Olave's Church at the far end of Gatcombe Road.

Building work began here in the 13th century on a chapel to serve the Estur family at Gatcombe House, which, along with its

The idylically-situated St Olave's Church at Gatcombe – which began life as a 13th century chapel for the powerful Estur family at Gatcombe House – remains as peaceful today as it was when Percy Stone produced this delightful sketch of it in the late-19th century.

manor, later passed to the great Worsley dynasty. St Olave's – dedicated for some unexplained reason to a 5th century Norwegian king notorious for his prosecution of the Christian faith – has undergone many alterations down the centuries. The 15th century was probably the work of the same masons who were employed during that period at Carisbrook Castle. The rebuilding of the porch in 1910 was the work of churchwarden Robert Urry, who constructed its rafters out of timbers from the warship *Thunderer*, which had fought alongside the *Victory* at the Battle of Trafalgar.

Inside the church lies the famously enigmatic effigy in oak of a crusader, regarded as old enough to be a memorial to one of the Estur family, though nobody has ever been able to pinpoint its precise origin. Its international fame can be ascribed to the imaginative Rev James Evans, rector here between 1965 and 1973, whose *Legend of Lucy Lightfoot* cast the Crusader and the eponymous heroine in an extraordinary time warp adventure which has intrigued a worldwide readership ever since the tale first appeared in booklet form. It still makes a useful contribution to the church's coffers.

On leaving the church, retrace your steps along Gatcombe Road as far as the turning providing access to Copsewood Cottage. Turn right here, following the route of footpath G6 to Carisbrooke. Initially gravel-surfaced, the climbing track becomes a concrete roadway for a short distance and then a rough-surfaced path for the steepest part of its ascent through a wood. Continue climbing to cross the route of another path (G10) and head northwards along the signposted Shepherds Trail, an ancient ridge path, soon passing through a metal gate.

Keeping the hedge and wall to your left, stay on the grass path, via another gate (left), and carry on, with the hedge switching to your right, into a dip and beyond the junctions with footpath N109 to Vayres and Cox's Corner (right). Shortly afterwards, your route takes you past another path, trailing in from the left. Further on, the path (now designated N108) runs into a shallow cutting, soon becoming overhung with vegetation as the cutting deepens and the path descends as a 'hollow-way' all the way to the road junction at Whitcombe Cross.

Turn left at the path's exit, then immediately left again, to descend the first part of a lane, looking out for the sign (right) indicating a footpath route to Carisbrooke Castle. With the castle clearly visible ahead, follow this path down and then up, bearing left as it climbs to emerge near the south-west corner of the castle walls. Go left, then right, alongside the castle moat – long since devoid of water – and walk the western perimiter until emerging, via a small gate, into the parking area nearest the castle keep (entrance).

In all its long history, the castle was attacked on only one occasion. The devastating French-led assault on the Isle of Wight in 1377, during the Hundred Years War, left the towns of Yarmouth, Francheville (Newtown) and, eventually, Newport, in ruins. Following their success, the raiders laid siege to the castle – the Island's last bastion of resistance. The fortress was well-defended under the resourceful command of Sir Hugh Tyrell, Captain of the Island, and, despite repeated attempts to storm it, the enemy forces were repelled.

Legend says that the French lost heart after their commander was mortally wounded by a crack shot from the 'silver bow' of Petrus de Heynoe (also recalled as Peter de Heyno), Lord of Stenbury, who was in charge of one of the nine local militia defending Carisbrooke. Look up to the west wall to a still prominent cruciform-shaped arrow slit. It's said to be the position from where de Heynoe took aim that fateful day. For centuries the slit has been known as Heynoe's Loope.

If de Heynoe was Carisbrooke's greatest hero, Charles I was certainly the castle's greatest – in terms of status – prisoner. Fearful of his future at the hands of the Commonwealth forces, the Stuart monarch took flight from Hampton Court in 1647 and sought sanctuary in the Isle of Wight. No doubt he expected a less than hostile reception from the Island's Governor, Colonel Robert Hammond who, although a Parliamentarian, opposed to the monarchy, was the brother of the King's chaplain. It was a difficult dilemma for Hammond. At first he welcomed Charles to Carisbrooke and the King was able to move freely around the Island as a guest of the Governor.

Leaving it was another matter. Despite the lack of restraint placed upon him, the King was effectively a prisoner at Carisbrooke. This prompted an arch Royalist, Captain John Burley, to engineer Charles's escape. The engineering was awful. The King became stuck in the bars of the window through which he was attempting to flee. He was found in this compromising situation by his jailer, whose comment later that he had come to pay his respects to Charles as he had heard he was leaving added irony to the farce! It led to a hardening of Parliamentary attitude. Hammond was forced to keep the King under much stricter lock and key. Two further attempts to free him were made. The first, though much better planned than Burley's botched effort, had much the same result. The King didn't get stuck in the window bars this time, but neither could he get through them.

Nitric acid was provided to him to aid his final bid for freedom, Whereas previously Charles had been housed in the Constable's Lodgings, he had by now been moved to a room in the castle's north curtain wall. The acid allowed him to cut through one of the window bars so that getting out was possible, but the plot was foiled by an informer before the time set for the escape. It was the beginning of the end for Charles I. In September 1648 he was taken to Newport and, two months later, the King began his fateful return to London. On 30 January 1649, Charles Stuart finally escaped his wordly torment at the hands of the executioner in Whitehall.

The finish point in the main car park is a few paces to the left.

Quarr and the Quarries –
the strength of the stone-built abbey

This 6-mile (9.6km) walk around the environs of Quarr Abbey begins in Ryde and takes you through its original suburb of Pelham Field, along the footpath route to the abbey, via Binstead, then inland on a combination of rural paths and quiet lanes to the edge of Wootton, returning via Ashlake Copse and Fishbourne. There are hills to encounter in Ryde and out in the countryside, but nothing too strenuous. The walk has only four stiles and follows a well-defined and signposted route.

Introduction: Without doubt, the original Cistercian abbey at Quarr was the most important ecclesiastical establishment ever built on the Isle of Wight. Between the 12th and 16th centuries it exercised power and influence over a wide area, well beyond the confines of the abbey complex itself. Fittingly, Quarr was also the site chosen by exiled Benedictine monks from France for their new abbey at the onset of the 20th century. The walk traces the origins and history of both, together with those of neighbouring Binstead and the limestone quarries from which the original abbey acquired its name.

The route also provides an insight into the early development of Ryde, from its beginnings as two distinct hill-divided hamlets to its status as a fashionable 'watering place' for England's aristocracy.

Parking and Public Transport: Immediate access to car parking in Ryde is available (for a fee) at the start point of the walk and on the other side of St Thomas' Street, a short distance up the road. Parking can also, of course, be found elsewhere in the town. The start point, just off the seafront at its western end, is a short walk from Island Line's Ryde Esplanade rail station (turn right on leaving it) and the adjacent bus station, with routes from all major Island destinations.

The proximity of both the cross-Solent Hovertravel terminal (for services from Southsea) and Ryde Pier (providing access to Wightlink's Fastcat ferry to/from Portsmouth Harbour) means the walk is well suited for a day's excursion from the mainland.

Information: With Ryde's seafront and town centre close to the start point, refreshment and toilet facilities are easily accessible. Quarr Abbey's tea garden, when open, offers a welcome refreshment stop *en route* while facilities are also available in Wootton village, via a short detour from the route. Further options are provided in the terminal area at Wightlink's Fishbourne car ferry terminal and at the nearby Fishbourne Inn.

Directions:

Start the walk at the entrance to the lower car park in St Thomas' Street. (grid ref SZ593929 – marked A on the route map). Go right, up the hill, following the road as it bends left, then turn right into Buckingham Road and stay with it as it bends left, uphill – following the signposted route of the Coastal Path. Turning right at the top of the hill, along the pavement, you soon pass the road sign (opposite West Street) that confirms you are in Spencer Road. Follow this pleasant road past the once grand villas of English nobility and the fine houses in between.

Ryde was a ferry port long before it was a town. Fishermen lived in shore-side cottages at what has been variously described as la Rye, la Riche or Ride. The name is derived from the Old English term for a small stream – a 'rith' or 'rithe' – and, in Ryde's case, the stream in question is the Monktonmead brook which still runs through it to the sea, though now largely underground. The fishermen supplemented their income by ferrying people across The Solent until the building of England's second longest pier, which started life in 1814 and was subsequently twice extended, enabled larger ferry-boars to call irrespective of the tide. There was another hamlet on the brow of the hill rising from the shore. The two settlements were eventually connected by the laying-out of Union Street, which is today still one of the town's principal shopping thoroughfares. Spencer Road. once magnificently lined with elm trees, runs through the first suburb – Pelham Field – and its grand houses recall the early ambitions of the town to enjoy the status of a 'watering place' to rival Brighton.

The very names Spencer Road and Buckingham Road are evocative of this era of pretension, though the villas built for the Duke of Buckingham and Earl Spencer, with grounds that swept down to the sea, are now inevitably divided into flats. The arched gateway at the entrance to the latter's Westfield Park remains an

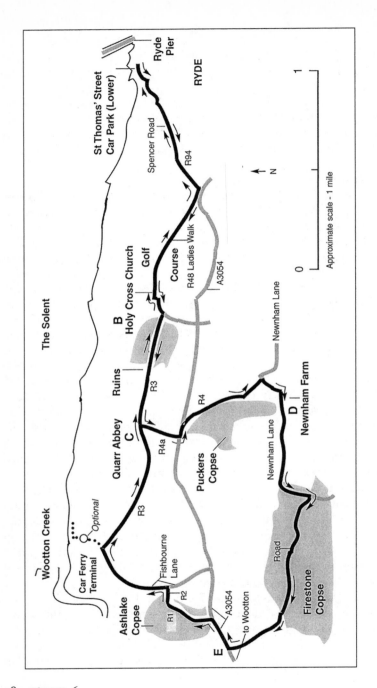

impressive feature. The house once boasted a sculpture gallery of fine Italian statuary, recalled by the stone-carved stag that still sits atop the archway, above the Latin motto *Qui Si Sans* (Here is Health). Picturesque Buckland Grange, further along, and just behind, the road, remains gabled in the Old English style with a bit of Gothic thrown in for good measure.

The road rises eventually to reach its termination at a metal barrier alongside the A3054, where the footpath sign (R94) points back to Ryde. Pass through the gap on the left and bear right to the start of footpath R48, signposted to Binstead and Quarr. Follow the tree-lined tarmac path – known as Ladies Walk – as it bisects the greens of Ryde Golf Club on its way down to a bridge across Binstead Brook, a former manorial boundary, where another path joins it (right) from Binstead shore. Climb the slope beyond the bridge and pass through the gap to the left of a wooden barrier onto a quiet section of road, bordered on the right by pleasant domestic architecture and then, Binstead's pretty Church of the Holy Cross (B on the map).

Guarded over by the Idol at the top, the former south entrance to Binstead Church, re-located to the churchyard boundary, has changed little since this drawing was made late in the 19th century.

Worth noting is the half-blocked arch set in the churchyard wall. Guarding over it, above the keystone, is a small, exceedingly ugly and much-weathered stone-carved figure of indeterminate gender. It's generally held to be a 'sheela-na-gig,' enigmatic effigies which suggest a link to fertility and may thus have a pagan origin. The precise origins of this grotesque, yet somehow endearing, little figure have long been a matter for debate – as has the precise identity of the creature upon whose head the sculpture squats, protected by a porch which looks as old as the figure but is, in fact. a much later addition. The porch is not the only protection extended to the sculpture. Binstead people have resisted its removal in the past, believing it brings them good fortune – or at least guards them against bad. They have a simple name for it – The Idol.

The arch is Norman and previously served as the north entrance to the church's former nave before re-location to its present site. This was centuries before Sir Thomas Hellyer's 1844 rebuilding of Holy Cross in the Old English style. Longer ago still, there may well have been a Saxon church on the site to serve the spiritual needs of the men who quarried the renowned Quarr-Binstead limestone, which was shipped across The Solent for use in the construction of Winchester Cathedral and a host of other notable structures. Transporting the stone was nothing like so much of an issue when it was utilised in the building of the nearby 12th century Cistercian abbey at Quarr.

Beyond the church, bear left with Church Road and then go right at the road junction a short distance further on. Just beyond a left-hand bend, leave the road to follow the route of bridleway R45, signposted to Quarr and Fisbourne. This wide track soon converts to a narrower path after veering left to the side of a house (Lingarth) and passing between posts. It bends right before forming a junction, via two more posts, with a tarmac track, also used by motor traffic.

Following the directional signs for the Coastal Path, bear right along the tree-lined route, passing Binstead Hall (right) before reaching the much newer housing of Abbots Close (left). The name serves as a reminder of the monastic establishment ahead – just as the house Macquarrie (right) recalls the origin of the name Quarr itself. Remains of the old stone quarries themselves are easy to spot on the left-hand side of the track. *The tarmac gives way to rougher path surfacing immediately beyond a gate across the road. Go through the smaller walker's gate on the left and follow the path*

The farmhouse at Quarr built out of remnants from the original Cistercian abbey following its demise by order of Henry VIII. Little has changed since the house was drawn by Percy Stone for a book on the Island's architectural antiquities in 1891.

through more open coastal countryside as it runs down to skirt the ruins of the medieval abbey (right). An information panel interprets both the visible remains and what has been lost (though this was missing itself early in 2004).

The abbey was founded in 1132 by Baldwin de Redvers, Earl of Devon and Lord of the Isle of Wight. For the next 400 years, until dissolution by Henry VIII, the monks at Quarr exercised considerable power and influence, with granges (farms) and other enterprises scattered throughout the Island. They came originally from a Benedictine house in Savigny, France, where a desire for a stricter code had led the community of monks, together with like-minded brothers from other French abbeys, to form the Cistercian order. Expansion followed, with Quarr one of the first Cistercian communities to be set up in England,

You can still see sections of the abbey's precinct walls. Most complete of the surviving buildings is a storehouse, since converted into a barn, but much of the stone from the dismantled abbey has long since been carted away for re-use in newer buildings.

The path now climbs past the farmhouse (a good example of the post-dissolution re-use of the old abbey's stone) *and two other semi-isolated cottages to reach the entrance to the medieval abbey's present-day successor (right – C on the map).* A tour of the abbey grounds, the gift shop and the idylically-situated tea garden is recommended.

A remarkable contrast to old Quarr's stone is provided by the striking red brick construction of the present abbey, which dates back to the start of the 20th century. The Benedictine community who first took up residence here, via a brief stay at Appuldurcombe House (see walk 10), were among those expelled from Normandy during religious persecution in 1901. New Quarr's church. conceived by the architect monk Dom Paul Bellot, is widely held to be a work of genius.

Turn left off the footpath (straight ahead if you have taken the opportunity to visit the abbey) and follow the main driveway to the A3054. Cross this busy road with care, then turn left to walk the full distance of the pavement alongside it, which provides access to the next section of the walk via a stile (right). Follow the well-trodden route of footpath R4 (signposted to Newnham Lane) along the side of a field until it bends right to another stile. This takes you through the pretty woodland of Puckers Copse.

According to legend (though it's challenged by the fact of her visible grave in the French abbey of Fontevrault), Eleanor of Aquitaine, rebellious wife of Henry II, lies buried beneath here in a golden coffin at the end of an underground passage. A magic spell protects it from intruders. The legend asserts that Eleanor, while she was imprisoned in the abbey at the King's behest, was insistent that the "melancholy boughs" around Quarr should be her final resting place. It is certainly true that Henry held her captive at various locations in the South, but no records exist to confirm that Eleanor was ever at Quarr. Yet, the legend persists – and the main road which divides the present abbey grounds from the copse is known to everyone on the Island at Elenor's Grove. The mis-spelling may be a serious matter for the troubled ghost of Eleanor reputedly haunts the copse.

Offering good views of Quarr's restored fish ponds (left), *path and copse end at a stile. Beyond it, bear slightly left up the sloping field, passing between trees, to exit via another stile. This takes you to the side of Newnham Lane. Go right here.* The road sees very little traffic but, as there is no footpath, caution is advised. *Stay with the undulating, winding route of the lane as it bends right on reaching Newnham Farm and descends a hill past the farmhouse (left – D on the map).* Newnham (formerly Ninham) was one of old Quarr's granges. Tenant farmers here long held the right to the first crop of hay in alternate years from the abbey's Monken Mede in present-day Ryde. Monken Mede became Monktonmead over time. The stream that ran through it adopted the name and, as explained, provided the origin for Ryde's.

The lane goes uphill and then down again. Eventually, after a sharp left-hand bend, it descends, twisting and turning, as it skirts Firestone Copse (right) to its junction with Firestone Copse Road. Go right here, staying close to the side of the road – which carries more traffic than Newnham Lane. Follow the winding route as it dissects the copse and eventually rises away from the woodland to continue between neat hedgerows as far as the modern housing development at Firestone Glade (right) and the final section downhill to a junction with the A3054 (E). Wootton Bridge, the creek and village amenities can be reached via a short detour to the left.

The walk route takes you right, uphill, alongside the main road to a point immediately before it bends right and descends away from Wootton. Cross the road here, using the traffic island, then go right and, soon afterwards, left, down Ashlake Copse Lane. Tarmac soon gives way to gravel, and then rough surface, as the path enters the copse, offering glimpses of Wootton Creek (left) before crossing a stream and rising to meet trackways serving the houses set amid this woodland environment.

Maintain your direction straight ahead as the tree-lined route, now on the flat, resumes the status of roadway and runs between housing before dipping and then rising to its junction (right) with footpath R1 – signposted as part of the Coastal Path – to Fishbourne. Take this narrow, tree-lined pathway between houses the short distance to the roadside at Fishbourne Lane. Cross the road with care – it's the route to and from the car ferry terminal and can be very busy at times – *and go left along the pavement, eventually passing the terminal (left). A short distance further on, opposite the Fishbourne Inn, go right to begin the signposted route of footpath R3 back to Quarr and Binstead* (although a short detour beforehand, beyond the footpath junction and down to the waterfront, will reward you with an aspect of Fishbourne in pleasant contrast to the hustle and bustle of the ferry terminal –

despite its proximity to it).

The Southern Railway developed the car ferry route to Portsmouth in 1927, changing dramatically the formerly sleepy environment of Fishbourne's haven-side hamlet, which had begun life centuries earlier as a 'fish house' for the monks at Quarr. The haven itself was, until relatively recently, referred to as Fish-house Creek or the Wootton River, Today's name combines the two as Wootton Creek.

Follow path R3 through a gate. It soon converts to true rural footpath status and takes you back to the abbey entrance at Quarr. From here, retrace your outward route back to Binstead, Ryde and the car park at St Thomas' Street.

Newport — Medieval tracks to a buried Roman past

This is essentially a walk through Newport town centre; short in distance – less than 2 miles (3.2km) – but extending a long way through the history of the Isle of Wight's capital. The only appreciable climbing on the route is the section in the residential area south of the town providing access to the Roman villa – the 20th century discovery of which forced a re-think on Newport's origins. It's a walk of contrasts. The bustling High Street, the town centre quayside, Church Litten's spacious park, quiet lanes and 'hide-away' footpaths all feature along its compact course.

Introduction: Newport was laid out as a medieval town. Its origins as such are easily traced via the surviving trackway routes – now busy streets at the core of today's town centre – which ran from Carisbrooke Castle down to the 'new port' at the navigable southern limit of the River Medina from The Solent. The town's subsequent history has been eventful, as befits its capital status, and not always triumphal. It was utterly devastated at the hands of French-led aggressors in the 14th century. Rebuilt, Newport has thrived at the heart of Island affairs – and sometimes those of the nation. The doomed Charles I, already in the hands of Cromwell's forces, made a final unsuccessful bid in Newport to negotiate his way out of trouble shortly before his execution in 1649.

Yet, there was an earlier chapter in the story of the town. The clues lay buried for nearly 2,000 years and then, in 1926, came the discovery that drew attention to its Roman past.

Parking and Public Transport: Newport lies at the hub of the Island, with main road connections in all directions. There are a number of town centre car parks. Drill Hall Road's is nearest to the start point of the walk, just a few paces away. Buses serve Newport town centre from all parts of the Island.

Information: Access to pubs, cafés, shops and public toilets is seldom more than a few minutes away from the route. The walk

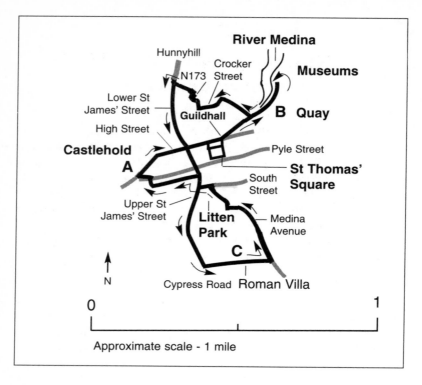

provides immediate access to three museums and the Roman villa.

Directions:

Begin the walk at the western end of Newport High Street (grid ref SZ496890 – A on the route map), just beyond the divergence of Pyle Street (the right fork as you face the town centre). This area is known as Castlehold.

The castle in question is, of course, nearby Carisbrooke. When the first of the Norman lords ruled the Island from Carisbrooke in the years following the 11th century Conquest, there was no town of Newport. A track ran eastwards from the castle down to the River Medina which, in an isle without roads, provided isolated Carisbrooke with its only outlet to the world beyond. The track forked as it neared the river. One route veered left to reach the Medina at it its limit of navigation by shipping. The track to the right ran as far as the first ford over the stream beyond the navigable river. The forked route survives today. The track to the left is now High Street; that to the right is Pyle Street. No explanation is needed for the naming of High Street. 'Pyle' may have been an early word for ford.

Newport's initial development straddled the tracks. Later, towards the end of the 12th century, Richard de Redvers, Earl of Devon and Lord of the Island, turned it into a proper town on the grid system, with new streets built at right-angles to High Street and Pyle Street. The walk ahead takes you along some that are still with us today. Castlehold, as the name implies, recalls the area of land retained by the governing de Redvers family for the use of the Lord of the Island at Carisbrooke. Up until the 19th century, Castlehold remained under the jurisdiction of its own Court Leet.

Follow High Street into the town's shopping centre, soon passing the Castle Inn (left), and carry on to reach the junction with St James' Street, with St James' Square on the right. Until 1926, the square was used for Newport's centuries-old cattle market before re-location in South Street. Unmoved by the passage of time is the conspicuous monument to Queen Victoria, whose close associations with the Isle of Wight via long residency at Osborne House have been well chronicled. Nearby is a bronze bust of Lord Louis Mountbatten, installed at Carisbrooke as Governor of the Isle of Wight in 1965 by the present queen, his niece, a post he still held at the time of his murder by Irish terrorists. The ancient post, effectively the continuation of the Norman lords, though long since stripped of the formidable powers they enjoyed, has never been filled since.

The multi-arched frontage of the former Isle of Wight Institution, designed by the great Regency architect John Nash, can be seen on the north-east corner of the square (ahead, right). It dates from 1811.

Continue along High Street for a short distance, as far as St Thomas' Square. Turn right and walk towards St Thomas' Church. Newport's most important church stands on the site of a much older predecessor, founded by Richard de Redvers around 1178 and dedicated to St Thomas a Becket. Seven subsequent centuries of use took their toll on the Norman church. Replacement began in 1854, when Prince Albert laid the foundation stone for the present church. Not many provincial churches can claim to be the final resting place of a royal Princess. St Thomas's at Newport is an exception.

Princess Elizabeth, second daughter of Charles I, was born in

1635. Intellectually gifted – at the age of eight she could read in French, Italian, Latin and Hebrew – she was a tragic victim of the turmoil in England at that time. After her mother and elder sister left the country at the start of the Civil War she never saw them again. Her father's dramatic fall-out with Parliament led, via a period of incarceration at Carisbrooke, to his execution in 1649. The future Charles II escaped the wrath of Cromwell's Commonwealth, but freedom eluded his little brother, Henry, Duke of Gloucester, and 14-year-old Elizabeth.

Parliament wanted them out of the way, fearing the Royalist cause would be re-ignited by their very presence. Henry and Elizabeth were banished to the country. Eventually, like their father before them, they were moved to Carisbrooke Castle in August 1650. There, they were treated courteously and with due respect, but Elizabeth's fragile heath – she was already suffering from ricketts and had always been a delicate child – quickly failed her at Carisbrooke. She contracted pneumonia after being caught in a shower on the castle's bowling green. On the morning of 8 September, Princess Elizabeth was found dead in her bed, "far removed from physicians and medical aid".

Princess Elizabeth's coffin was placed in a vault inside the old St Thomas' Church. The brass plate affixed to it was not a new one. The church authorities simply reversed and re-used a plate originally produced for a former Minister of Newport. This final indignity was eventually rectified by Queen Victoria at the time of the present church's construction. Shocked that no memorial had ever been put up to the memory of the tragic princess, Victoria commissioned a magnificent sculptured monument above the re-located tomb. It can be seen at the head of the church's north aisle. By Royal command, the windows on the north wall near the monument were filled with stained glass so that only a gentle light should fall on Elizabeth's tomb.

Turn left before the war memorial to walk alongside the south wall of the church. The restaurant ahead of you on the right, with its prominent Georgian bow window frontage is one of Newport's architectural treasures. God's Providence House is not called that by chance or whim. The tablet above its entrance bears the date 1701, but this may refer to a partial rebuilding in that year rather than the date of actual construction. Whatever the truth of that, the site occupied by the building has a special place in the town's history as the place where an outbreak of plague was finally tamed in 1584 after an 18-month rampaging march of misery through Newport. "God's providence is my inheritance," reads the inscription which accompanies the date and explains the name. Opinions vary as to whether this was the last house to record a plague death at Newport in 1584 or one of the few – possibly the only one – in which nobody died.

Turn left again and walk the short distance to rejoin High Street. Cross the road with care and bear right into Quay Street – the final section of the original trackway route to the navigable Medina. Watchbell Lane (left, to the side of Calvert's Hotel) recalls Newport's evening curfew bell, signalling to all townsfolk the need to extinguish the fire in their home – and lessen the risk of fire in their town.

The imposing building on the right is Newport Guildhall, which now houses the Museum of Island History. Originally known as the Town Hall, it was built in 1813 to another of John Nash's designs, a work of elegant symmetry. Newport was fortunate in having Nash – whose magnificent decoration of the Regency period

Early-19th century engraving of John Nash's Town Hall (later Guildhall) at Newport – before the addition of the disfiguring clock tower. the view is from High Street. to the left if Quay Street, providing access to the harbour.

included Regent Street, Regent's Park, Clarence House and Brighton Pavilion – so close to hand at East Cowes Castle, his principal Isle of Wight home. Many think the town should have demonstrated a good deal more respect for his memory when, at the other end of the century, the Corporation commissioned the disfiguring addition of the Guildhall's clock tower as a commemoration of Queen Victoria's Golden Jubilee. So much for symmetry.

Walk down Quay Street to reach its 'T' junction with Sea Street. Cross the road and continue straight ahead to pass under the road bridge onto Newport Quay (B on the map). Follow the quayside road past the Riverside Centre. Still the furthest point of navigation on the Medina from Cowes, the harbour remains active, though devoted more these days to the upkeep and winter quartering of yachts. Many of its former warehouses have been converted for new use, notably the old grain store which since 1997 has been home to the Isle of Wight Bus Museum's impressive collection of vehicles, and, further on (right), the Classic Boat Museum, a fascinating collection of historic small craft and maritime memorabilia.

Turn round at the boat museum and retrace your steps back into Sea Street. Turn right to go past the Quay Arts Centre – a further imaginative re-use of former commercial buildings – and walk its full length to the junction with Holyrood Street.

On the corner (right) is the Railway Medina pub, the only visible reminder that this was formerly the approach to Newport station, hub of a once extensive network of steam-worked railways that ran throughout the Island. A succession of Increasingly controversial line closures began in the early-Fifties and culminated, after a titanic struggle to keep Newport on the rails, in the departure of the last trains to Cowes and Ryde in February 1966. The traffic-choked roads that feed into Newport's Coppins Bridge roundabout today are evidence enough of the short-sighted folly.

Feasibility studies have demonstrated the economic and social worth of re-opening the principal link to Ryde. It will surely happen one day – but the station won't be on the same site. Cross Holyrood Street and look to the left of the pub, up the slope to the nearest thing the Isle of Wight has to a motorway. That's where the trains used to stop. Even modern trams would baulk at the prospect now.

Facing the pub, go right up Holyrood Street and take the first right turn into Crocker Street. Two-thirds of the way along, turn right again into St Cross Lane. Before there was Newport, there was St Cross Priory, founded early in the 12th century on the banks of the Medina's Lukely Brook tributary by a community of French monks from the abbey of Tiron. Thus we have the explanation for the naming of Holyrood Street, on the route of the former track that provided access to the priory. Nothing remains of the abbey today – it was ironically destroyed by the French in 1377, as they laid waste to the entire town, and never fully recovered – and there's very little left of St Cross Mill, one of the five Lukely water mills – a remarkable number for such a short stream. The remnant lies ahead of you.

A short distance from the road junction, fork left, then go right to follow the zig-zag route of footpath N173 (signposted to Hunnyhill). It takes you past the surviving mill buildings – note the old paving. *The footpath emerges alongside Lukely Brook. Carry on along the path, past its junction with footpath N34 (right) and go up to the side of Hunny Cross Lane, just short of its junction with Hunnyhill.* This location has for centuries been known as Towngate, the bridged entrance to Newport from the north.

Go left to reach the junction. The railway to Yarmouth and Freshwater used to cross Hunnyhill on Towngate Viaduct, just to the right of the present road junction, until it was axed in 1953. *Go left again to cross Lukely Brook on Towngate Bridge at the foot of Hunnyhill, which immediately becomes Lower St James' Street as you walk towards the town centre.*

On the corner of Lugley Street (second right) stands the former Newport Grammar School, which dates from the early-17th century. Thirty-odd years after its construction came the event with which it is most closely associated, when a beleaguered, captive Charles I hopelessly tried to preside over the culmination of negotiations with his Commonwealth adversaries. The Treaty of Newport was a misleading title for the piece of paper over which the two sides haggled. There never was a treaty. Charles was a loser by that time. A Royal loser's ultimate fate then was to lose your head.

Arriving at the junction with High Street, cross the road with care into St James' Square and carry on in the same direction beyond the South Street junction (left) and the George Inn (right), now following Upper St James' Street southwards. Stay with it beyond the junctions with Orchard Street (left) and Trafalgar Road (right), just opposite, Nodehill Middle School.

Formerly the town's library. the school stands in what is still known locally as Nodehill. The word 'noddy' seems to have been mainly used as a term of abuse on the Isle of Wight, usually denoting an idiot. Tradition asserts that Islanders reserved it especially for the French. A band of Frenchmen, retreating from the failed 1377 siege of Carisbrooke Castle (see walk 5), were ambushed and slaughtered in a narrow lane north-east of the castle. Islanders took delight thereafter in referring to the event as The Battle of the Noddies. The lane in which it is supposed to have taken place became known as Deadman's Lane – renamed Trafalgar Road after Nelson's victory in 1805.

Use the pedestrian crossing ahead to reach the far side of Medina Avenue and continue in the same direction up the hill beyond it (St John's Road). Ignore all turns-off until you reach the junction (left) with Cypress Road. Take this turning and walk down the hill, passing the junctions with Mount Pleasant Road and Wykeham Road (both on the left), then Queens Road to reach Newport Roman villa (left), the entrance to which is set back from the road (C on the map).

The villa's re-discovery was not made until 1926 – during the sinking of foundations for a garage. Excavation revealed extensive remains of what is believed to be a late Romano-British farmhouse dating back to 280 AD, when it would have stood at the centre of an extensive country estate sloping down to the river, right at the heart of the Island. Newport may be a medieval town, but this is proof that the Romans were here first.

Leaving the villa, resume the walk downhill to the foot of Cypress Road, then turn left into Medina Avenue. Passing two road junctions (left), follow the road as it bends sharp left at the junction with St George's Approach. Just before the junction (right) with Church Litten, use the pedestrian crossing to reach the far side of the road, turn into Church Litten and, immediately afterwards, use a second controlled crossing to the pavement skirting the boundary of Litten Park. Cut across the park to join the pathway running through it and go right. Further on, alongside the present library (left), either fork left to exit the park via the monument to Valentine Gray, or take the path further right to leave it beneath the stone-built arched entrance.

The 12th century St Thomas a Becket Church was built as a dependant chapel of Carisbrooke, where all burials took place. This remained the situation until the devastating late-16th century plague left Newport with too many dead bodies to cart off over the

The ornate stone-built gateway to the burial ground at Church Litten, Newport, pictured late in the 19th century. The area is a public park today but the old gateway survives.

rough tracks to Carisbrooke's graveyard. The solution lay with the conversion of the town's archery butts into a new burial ground on the then outskirts of the town. This became known as Church Litten. The final interment took place here in 1858 and, in 1930, Church Litten was laid out as the parkland it is today (see plaque).

Some memorials remain – and none more poignant than that to the little chimney sweep, Valentine Gray. It was erected at the expense of local people appalled at Valentine's short, tragic life amid the choking soot of the Newport's chimneys he was forced to climb. The appalling work and harsh treatment he was made to suffer did have a positive outcome. It was instrumental in the passing of reform legislation in Parliament which abolished for ever the use of children as chimney sweeps.

Leaving the park, continue straight ahead as far as South Street, then turn left and walk to the junction with Upper St James' Street (opposite the George Inn). Using the pedestrian crossing, bear right to pass the McDonalds restaurant, then go left into Scarrots Lane, passing the rear of Chapel Street car park at the far end (left). Go right at the 'T' junction into New Street and, soon afterwards, turn left into Pyle Street to complete the last few paces of the walk back to the junction with High Street.

Medieval Boroughs – the port that grew from the Thorley silt

The next two walks together provide a long circular ramble around the rural West Wight, linking the medieval boroughs of Yarmouth and Newtown. It is suggested that each walk is done separately, using the bus service along the A3054 (see details below) from or to Shalfleet, midway point between the two. This outward leg of the walk extends 6 miles (9.6km), starting with a tour of Yarmouth's compact town centre and then heading along the quiet north-western coastline up to Hamstead and then down to Shalfleet. Beyond Yarmouth, much of the route in the countryside follows the Island's well-defined Coastal Path along footpaths and tracks. A limited amount of roadside walking is involved and stiles are encountered on the rural section.

Introduction: All things are relative. Yarmouth is old, certainly, but it's nothing like as old as Thorley, a mile or so inland, and it's the history of Thorley that must first be considered when assessing the origins of Yarmouth. The Celts may have known Thorley. The Romans definately did. They knew it as a port, tucked comfortably away on the estuary of what would later be called the western River Yar. Over the centuries, the estuary gradually silted up so that Thorley became increasingly difficult to reach by ship. The obvious solution was to locate a new landing place nearer the coast, at the mouth of the river. Inevitably, around the new port a settlement developed and prospered.

Its name was Ermud, which later evolved into Eremue, under which guise it was laid out in the middle years of the 12th century as the Island's first planned medieval town. We know it today as Yarmouth.

Parking and Public Transport: Yarmouth's principal road link is the A3054 from Ryde and Newport, from which there is easy, signposted access to the large car park south of the Yar Bridge and adjacent to the bus station, start point for the walk. The town's main bus services are provided by routes 7 and 7A from Ryde and

Newport (and also round the coast from the south of the Island). Circular route 15 (West Wight Tour) starts and finishes at the bus station in summer, as does the open-top service 42 to and from The Needles Battery. There is also a daily morning service in the summer from Newport to Yarmouth along route 47, which runs via Thorness Bay and Newtown.

Information: Yarmouth has a full range of town centre facilities (pubs, cafés, shops and toilets) within easy reach of the bus station. Once out of the town, all amenities are conspicuous by their absence until arrival at Shalfleet's New Inn (although a fairly short detour straight ahead from Ningwood Bridge, then right, alongside the main road, will take you to that village's Horse and Groom pub).

Directions:
Begin the walk from the town end of Yarmouth bus station (grid ref SZ353898 – marked A on the route map) by turning left at the telephone kiosk and heading for the Wightlink ferry terminal, a short distance away. The mouth of the western Yar lies directly opposite that of the Lymington River on the mainland. There is a long history of seaborne communication between the two, dating at least back to the days of the Roman port at Thorley. Sail and oar powered the boats until 1830, when the SS *Glasgow* began a regular passenger service between Yarmouth and Lymington. Subsequent ownership and operation by a succession of railway undertakings eventually saw the post-war construction of a new slipway to accommodate the double-ended roll on-roll off ferries needed to transport motor vehicles as well as passengers. With their arrival on the scene, Yarmouth's ferry terminal moved from the pier to its present location.

Go right immediately before the ferry terminal to pass the town's lifeboat station (right) and the entrance to Yarmouth Castle (left), one of several Tudor fortifications in the Solent area developed for Henry VIII. The square castle, surrounded on two sides by the sea, represented the very latest in military engineering when it was completed in 1547, three years after a particularly serious French raid on the Island's north coast. The castle's garrison reached its peak at the time of the Civil War – 70 men in 1654 – but a year after the Restoration of 1660, the swollen force was disbanded. By 1669, when Admiral Sir Robert Holmes was

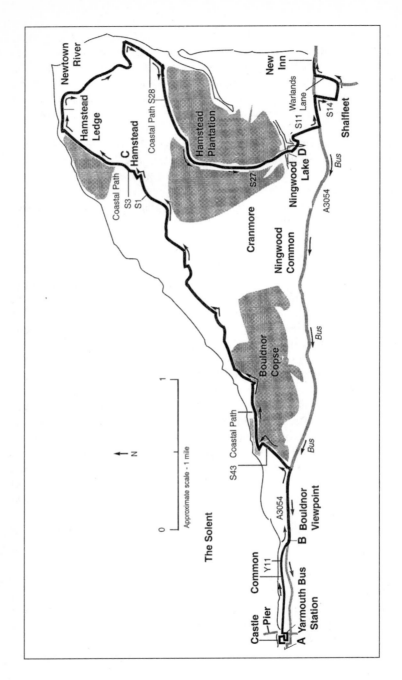

appointed Captain of the Island, the Tudor castle was manned again, but only by a small garrison of four gunners. It was outmoded and ill-equipped to fulfil the job for which it had been built.

Undertaking, on his own initiative, to reorganise the Island's defence, Holmes reduced the castle to a more manageable size by demolishing the earthworks, filling in the moat – and building a house right alongside it. It's now the George Hotel. The old castle entrance was blocked, a new one replaced it on the south side (where it remains today) and the castle's guns were concentrated on the seaward side, augmented by a new battery on the quay.

Not a lot happened to, or at, Yarmouth Castle in the century or so that followed. The garrison force remained constant (a captain, a master gunner and five ordinary gunners – nothing like enough to man the ordnance without the help of the local militia) and not even the great Napoleonic Wars shook the modest castle out of its slumber. The 19th century did see some repairs, modifications and armament renewal, but in 1885 came the decision to withdraw the garrison for good and dismantle the castle's guns. There was some, very limited, military use in both World Wars. Then, in the Fifties, the old Tudor fortress was finally available for rehabilitation and eventual public access as an historical monument. The castle has been in the care of English Heritage since 1984 and is open to the public between April and October.

Carry on to reach the town square, with the pier and adjacent car park to your left. Yarmouth Pier, built entirely of timber, has changed little since it was opened in 1876, extending 685 feet out to sea, primarily to meet the cross-Solent ferries from Lymington. Within a matter of weeks, 150 feet of deck had been smashed to bits after the pleasure steamer *Prince Leopold* crashed into it in broad daylight and the finest of weather. An apology was due. It came not from the ship's owners but from the Corporation of Yarmouth, anxious not to fall out at so early a stage of the pier's existence with the very people who were bringing the trade – and revenue – necessary to keep it viable! Equipped with its tiny pavilion (originally the pier-master's office) in 1927, the pier, as noted, lost commercial importance with the opening of the new car ferry terminal. The vessels that call today are modest by comparison to the old paddlers, but the pier has undergone extensive restoration in recent years, thanks to a committed Yarmouth Harbour Commission, which recognises its value to the port.

Yarmouth's town square. The 17th century St James' Church is seen on the left, with Yarmouth Town Hall in the right foreground. A tour of the compact medieval town is part of the walk itinerary.

Go right, soon passing Yarmouth Town Hall. Yarmouth was granted its first town charter by Baldwin de Redvers, Lord of the Island, around 1135. A second followed in 1334, by which time the town's status as a borough had been enhanced by the right to elect its own representative to Parliament. By 1440, it had the powers to elect a Mayor. Parliamentary representation was increased to two in 1584. All these key dates are well documented. Yet, the date of the Town Hall's construction remains something of a mystery. It certainly wasn't there in 1272, when the site it occupies was used as a market place. Possibly, the Town Hall was part of Yarmouth's rebuilding following the disastrous attack by French-led forces in 1377, when the town was largely destroyed by fire. One thing we can be certain of – the building was completely renovated in 1763.

Yarmouth began unravelling as a town of status with the passing of the Reform Act of 1832, which stripped it of the right to its own MPs. In 1901 the town lost its borough status altogether after unsuccessfully petitioning Queen Victoria for a new charter. Yet, while the Isle of Wight Council now dispenses unitary authority across the length and breadth of the Island, Yarmouth retains a town council. Its members deal with parochial matters only – but they still meet in the Town Hall.

Explore the compact town centre, which retains much of its medieval origins, by *turning right again, along the lane leading to the Wheatsheaf Inn. Go left here, into Wheatsheaf Lane, and left again along Bridge Road* (leading to the Yar Bridge across the estuary, built in 1860 and modernised in recent years), *which returns you to the square, with St James's Church opposite.* Work on the present church began in 1614, replacing buildings mauled by the French. Its principal feature of interest is a white marble statue of Sir Robert Holmes. As he was one of Yarmouth's most prominent personalities, it seems fitting that Holmes should be so splendidly recalled here. However, while the head of the sculpture is a true representation of the Admiral, the body is that of King Louis XIV of France! Holmes captured the statue at sea, ordering that the King's head be removed and replaced with his own.

Turn left and then right into High Street, a fascinating mix of commercial and (increasingly as you proceed) domestic architecture. *Walk its full length, passing the junctions with South Street and Baskets Lane (right)* and enjoying frequent glimpses of the nearby Western Solent in between (left), *to emerge at the start of Yarmouth Common. Follow the route of footpath Y11a (part of the Coastal Path), signposted to Bouldnor, Hamstead and Shalfleet. It takes you along the seawall for the length of the Common and beyond it, dropping to a lower level via steps and becoming less structured before rising again for its final section. Just before the end of the seawall, bear left, up a winding path, to the car park at Bouldnor Viewpoint, off the A3054 (B on the map).*

Using the pavement, go left along the road, passing Eastmore Court and Port La Salle – from where the pavement is replaced by a dwindling grass verge – until reaching a junction with a gravel-surfaced lane, the route of the next section of Coastal Path (footpath S43), signposted to Hamstead and Shalfleet. Pleasantly bordered by trees, the lane ends at the driveway to Byways (right), your route continuing via footpath S1 (look for signpost) through woodland. Following left and sharp right turns in quick succession, the path twists and turns between trees close to the shore (left). On reaching a path junction, carry on straight ahead, soon skirting the water's edge. The path now turns inland. Bear right through the woodland and then follow the path round a left turn, heading again towards the sea. This soon brings you to a Coastal Path diversion sign.

Follow the signposted path route, bordered by the shore and trees, across a bridge and into woodland, your course marked by an old concrete War Department artillery stone in the middle of the path. It's a reminder of your proximity to the former Bouldnor battery, alone among the coastal batteries on the Island's north coast in being specifically constructed for Second World War use. *Stay with the well-defined route as it emerges from the trees – with a conifer plantation ahead, on the right – and continues to a sign confirming that S1 is now following a permanent path diversion. Bear right along its signposted route to Shalfleet, via Hamstead and the Newtown River, as it turns away from the coast into another wooded area and runs to a gate alongside a sign identifying the adjoining woodland as the Forestry's Commission's Bouldnor Forest plantation.*

The waymarked path now takes you into more open countryside, offering views of the downland scenery to the right. *before running again into woodland (huts on left). Bear left past the entrance to two houses, then go right, following the signposted S1 route along a gravel-surfaced lane (West Close), which provides access to homes on either side. Turn left at the 'T' junction, following the directional sign* (which shows that you have travelled 2.5 miles since leaving Yarmouth) *into the rough-surfaced, tree-lined Sea View Road.*

Still following the signposted and waymarked route of path S1, turn right along the track that also serves as the driveway to Cliff Cottage, then go through a waymarked metal gate and continue the walk down a grass path to a stile. From here, the route skirts a field, following a line of small trees (left), with houses beyond them, before bearing left, as the Coastal Path sign indicates. Cross the wide expanse of open land to a stile on the right, then follow the path through a metal gate – taking note of the signs warning of the electrified fence ahead of you. Carry on in the same direction, with the route now bordered by the fence (right) and a hedge (small trees).

On a clear day, there are good views from here of The Solent and the Hampshire coastline beyond it. *Bear left with the field boundary and look for a stile in the hedgerow. Beyond it, bear left to another stile, marked by a footpath directional sign. Ignoring the route (right) of path S30, stay with the Coastal Path route – now designated S3 – to reach Lower Hamstead. The path takes a series of turns – left, right, left and right again – before joining a track,*

John Nash designed his house at Hamstead as a 'cottage style' manor. The
building, pictured in 1835, was extensively altered by him in later years.

*bordered by a fence (left) and a hedge, with Grange Cottage on the
right.*

Hamstead (C on the map) was one of the great Cistercian
abbey of Quarr's outlying granges (see walk 6). Henry VIII's
dissolution of the monasteries passed it from Abbey to Crown, and
then into private ownership. Outwardly, nothing much changed
until 1806, when the land was bought by the architect John Nash.

While retaining East Cowes Castle as his principal Island home,
Nash transformed Hamstead by rebuilding its dilapidated
farmhouse and significantly extending the estate. He also founded
a brickworks – it is still possible to find examples of its output on
the beach – and built the Island's first recorded railway, a circular
narrow gauge system, to serve it. Following Nash's death in 1835,
his wife, Mary, retired to Hamstead and the estate eventually passed
to her relatives, the Pennethornes, who built the present Hamstead
Grange in the 1880s to the south of the villa developed by Nash.
Sadly, little remains of the architect's fine house today and the
Hamstead estate has reverted fully to its former peaceful self.

Unbelievably – and that really is the only adequate term – it was poised on the very brink of disaster in the 1960s when plans, thankfully thwarted, were announced to site a nuclear power station right outside the Grange!

Carry on through Hamstead Farm before turning right (through the gate or over the stile) to follow the signposted Coastal Path route down to the shore at Hamstead Ledge. The sea glimpses through the trees on the left and the wide open countryside panorama to the far-off Downs on the right add enchantment to the descent to what is just about the quietest of all the Island's beaches, devoid of all the usual seaside facilities. It's very remoteness should be refreshing enough – but it has not always been as peaceful as this. To the left of the beach as you face the sea (best reached from the path on the way down) is the incongruous sight of a concrete ramp. It was built during the Second World War as part of the extensive training carried out along the Island coast for the D-Day landings in Normandy.

Follow the trodden route of the path as it skirts the shore – passing the little memorial (set back on the right) to local victims of early 20th century sea tragedies – *as far as a footpath direction sign, indicating the next section of path S3 away from the shore towards Lower Hamstead and Shalfleet. It takes you up the incline, with the aid of steps, over a stile and along a narrow, but pretty, waymarked path between hedges and trees.*

The next part of the route, out in the open, is on a lengthy section of raised duck-boarding – effectively a bridge – spanning one of the many inlets of the adjacent Newtown Estuary. It takes you to another stile. Beyond it, bear left across a field – the route is usually easy to make out – to a further stile between trees, then bear right to follow the trodden path along the field boundary before it adopts a meandering route, partly on duck-boarding, in making a broad left turn at the water's edge.

Eventually, the path bends right onto higher, dryer ground, twisting through a clump of small trees and bushes to a stile, then resumes its route eastwards (left) alongside a field to reach a stile providing access to the quayside on the west bank on the Newtown River. Go right here, along a rough-surfaced lane, following the signposted route to Shalfleet past the isolated homes and farm buildings of Lower Hamstead. The path – now designated S28 (part of both the Coastal Path and Hamstead Trail) – skirts fields, native trees and, finally, the towering conifers of the Forestry Commission plantation on its way to a trackway 'T' junction at the edge of Cranmore's delightfully eccentric village. – a sort of up-market shanty town without a trace of tarmac.

Go *left here, following the signposted Coastal Path route towards Main Road. Ignore the Hamstead Trail's right turn a short distance further on* (which leads into the heart of Cranmore). *Stay with the track as it threads its way between the conifers and eventually breaks free to cross the delightful bridge at Ningwood Lake (D).* This is truly an idyllic location, whether the tide is high or low. *Immediately after crossing the bridge, look out for footpath S11 (left), signposted to Main Yarmouth-Newport Road, a quarter-of-a-mile away.*

Follow this path on the fringe of woodland (right) as it descends to the waterside and then bears left to cross an inlet of Ningwood Lake on a planked bridge. The path beyond the bridge climbs to a sharp right turn, then descends to follow a meandering route to a hedge which separates it from the A3054 Newport-Yarmouth road (right). Stay with the path as it bends left and climbs alongside the hedge to reach a stile (right). Cross the stile to the side of the main road, bear left and use the grass verge as far as Shalfleet House (left). Cross the road at this point, with care, to a stile marking the start of a signposted footpath.

The path skirts new housing (left) before it bends left to a footpath sign at the the side of a lane. Cross this quiet road and turn left, following its winding route through a residential area on the edge of Shalfleet village and past the village shop/post office (right). Converted from a milking parlour, the shop is well worth a visit as it retains clear evidence of its former use! *Ignoring turns-off, carry on until the lane* (the street sign identifies it at this point as Warlands Lane) *reaches a 'T' junction with the A3054. Cross the main road when it is safe to do so, then go right, down the hill, using the grass verge to reach the New Inn (left – D on the map).* which more than once in recent times has been voted the Isle of Wight's family pub of the year.

The nearest bus stops for the journey back to Yarmouth, or in the opposite direction, are both near the pub.

Medieval Boroughs – retracing history in the Newtown of old

The continuation of the cross-country route linking the two former medieval boroughs in West Wight takes you from Shalfleet up to the former town and seaport of Newtown, now the most tranquil of villages, then back to Shalfleet and on to Yarmouth on a wide sweep via Newbridge, Wellow and Thorley. Virtually the entire 10-mile (16km) route follows rural footpaths, with limited roadside walking involved. The paths are mostly well-defined – waymarked by a variety of means – and avoid any steep climbing. There are, however, a large number of stiles, especially between Shalfleet and Newbridge. If you enjoy quiet, contemplative walking, this one's for you!

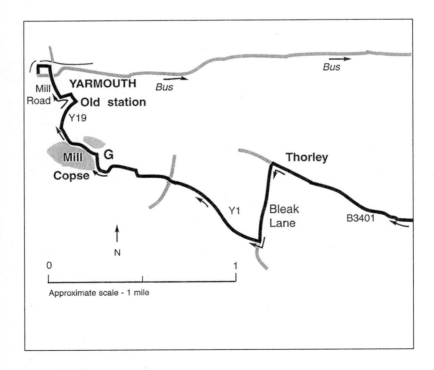

Introduction: The contrast between modern-day Yarmouth and Newtown could hardly be more profound. While the former has survived intact the rigours of centuries, essentially the same medieval town, Newtown offers only tantalising glimpses (notably at the late-17th century town hall) of its former status. Yarmouth is the western stepping-off point for cross-Solent travellers. Newtown is a reserve for birds in transit. Once a Parliamentary borough, electing two Members of Parliament, it elects now to remain about as far removed as possible from the strains of 21st century life.

Its history lies, for the most part, hidden, but it can be traced and this walk sets out to uncover the ghosts of the past. Vulnerable Newtown, a magnet for invasion, is now well off the beaten track. Totally at peace.

Parking and Public Transport: See outward leg details (walk 8) for information on the bus services linking Yarmouth with Shalfleet. If you opt to drive to Shalfleet and return by bus from Yarmouth (rather than the other way round), free car parking is available in Mill Lane, near the resumption point for the route up to Newtown.

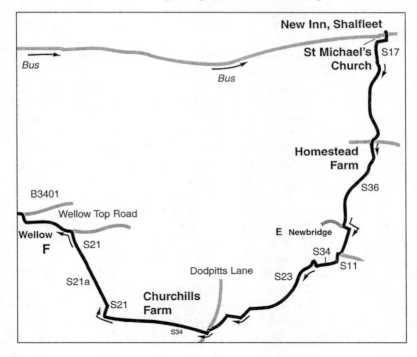

Don't confuse it with the parking area for the New Inn, immediately beyond the pub. The public car park is further up the lane, on the left-hand side.

Information: Shalfleet's pub and the village stores (see walk 8) offer the only facilities on the route until arrival back at Yarmouth (save for the village shops on the approach to the town). Present-day Newtown has fresh air and tranquility in abundance – but no amenities of any sort.

Directions:

Picking up the route at the New Inn (grid ref SZ414893 – marked A on the route map), turn left immediately beyond the pub into Mill Lane. Go past Shalfleet Manor Farm (right) and, further along, the public car park (left). Just beyond the latter, fork right down the delightfully tranquil Mill Road, passing Shalfleet Mill (right), now a private residence, crossing the adjacent stream on a bridge and entering the woodland beyond. Follow the path as it climbs to veer right. Immediately before the metal farm gate ahead, with the entrance to a house on your right, go left and walk up the path – the grass surface giving way to tarmac – to emerge at the roadside. Bear left, then cross to the other side of the road to continue the walk.

Although there is relatively little traffic. the road has no proper footpath, just a grass verge, so care is needed – particularly when *crossing the road again to a gate providing access to a section of off-road pathway. Follow the path's waymarked route right, alongside the hedge, eventually passing through a swing gate and veering right again to reach a second gate and the path's exit alongside a roadside bus stop. Bear left here, then sharp left, following the signposted route to Old Town Hall along peaceful Town Lane as far as a bridge.*

This is Newtown or Cassies Bridge (B on the map). You'll probably want to stop awhile to soak up the sheer beauty of this peaceful location and perhaps study the fascinating variety of building material used in the old bridge's construction and subsequent maintenance. *Having crossed the bridge, look out for a stile and footpath sign on the left. Take this path as it turns immediately to the right and follows the water's edge (Causeway Lake) to another stile. Carry on straight ahead, eventually bearing right, immediately after bushes, to climb gently through a meadow to a wooden swing gate. Beyond the gate, the path runs through a*

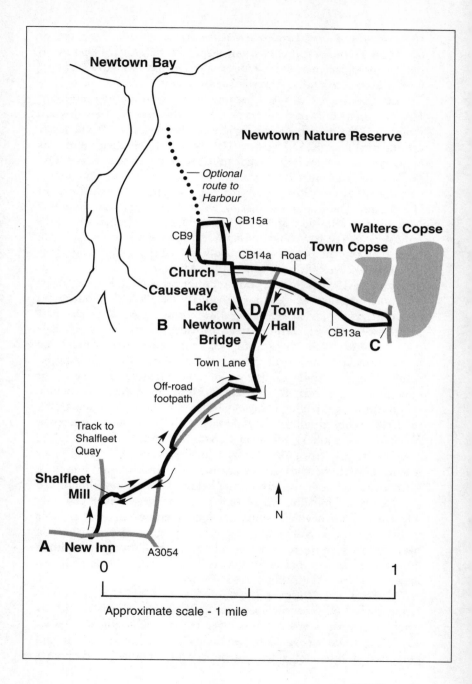

Newtown Bay

Newtown Nature Reserve

Optional route to Harbour

CB15a

CB9

CB14a   Road

Walters Copse

Town Copse

Church

Causeway Lake

B

D   Town Hall

CB13a

C

Newtown Bridge

Town Lane

Off-road footpath

Track to Shalfleet Quay

Shalfleet Mill

N

A   New Inn   A3054

0   1

Approximate scale - 1 mile

short section of woodland to arrive at what was formerly the site of the town pound in once bustling medieval Newtown. There's no bustle about the place these days. Present-day Newtown is just about the quietest village on the Isle of Wight.

Exactly when Newtown became 'new' is difficult to pinpoint. Early records confirm that it was part of the manor of Swainston, which was granted by King Egbert to the Bishop of Winchester around the year 826. Evidence is lacking on whether there was actually a settlement here at that time, or at any time over the next 400 or so years before the first charter of which any record remains was granted in 1256 by Aymer de Valence, Bishop-elect of Winchester. The one thing missing from the charter was the name Newtown. It referred instead to Francheville, the original title. This indicated a 'free town' where land and tenements were held at a fixed rent and the people were mostly free of the usual obligations to perform services for the Lord of the Manor.

Francheville developed, and no doubt prospered, because of its proximity to the sea. Its port rivalled those of Yarmouth and Newport, and may at one stage have been regarded as the pre-eminent of the three. Yet, disaster was waiting in the wings. A little over a century after the granting of that first charter, French-led forces attacked the north coast of the Island with devastating results. Foreign raids on the vulnerable offshore isle were not uncommon – far from it. Some authorities suggest that Francheville was burnt by rampaging Danes in 1001. Yet, the scale of the attack in 1377 eclipsed all others. Along with Yarmouth, and then Newport (see walk 5), Francheville was laid to waste.

The tragedy has given rise to a local version of the Pied Piper legend (indeed, there are strong grounds for believing that it may be the *original* version, conceived long before Robert Browning linked it so firmly to Hamelin). Plague-carrying rats were almost certainly a factor in Francheville's demise. A decimated population was able to offer only token resistance against the aggressors. This was a blow from which the town never fully recovered, though rebuilding did eventually take place. So was it Newtown that emerged as a 'new town' from the rubble of 1377's disaster?

History is seldom as straightforward as that. In fact, Francheville and Newtown seem to have co-existed side-by-side as place-names for centuries. Whatever name it was going by post-1377, the town struggled to regain its former prosperity. It still possessed a safe and active harbour, and remained a corporate

Newtown's surviving Town Hall, built at the end of the 17th century, recalls the present 'hide-away' village's former status as a medieval borough and seaport. The other relics of the past are harder to find in this quietest of places.

town, but the seeds of long, drawn-out decline had been sown. Nobody, however, could have guessed it would go as far as it did.

By Newtown standards, the Church of the Holy Spirit, ahead of you on the right, is hardly old at all. It wasn't built until 1836, but it does occupy an ancient ecclesiastical site. Little is known of the original church, dedicated to St Mary Magdalene, but the assumption is that it was founded in the 13th or 14th centuries. That raises the intriguing question – was it there when the French attacked in 1377?

Street names are conspicuous by their absence in what remains of Newtown, but are included below for historical interest.

Unless you opt first for a walk past the relatively modern cottages in High Street (right) to inspect the restored village pump, *carry on down the road ahead (Church Street). Stay with it as it bends left (Key Street) and eventually reaches its termination at a small roadside parking area. Just beyond, go through a swing gate to take footpath CB9, signposted to The Harbour and providing access to Newtown Nature Reserve.*

Emerging through a second gate into a field, walk down the slope, keeping the hedge to your right, and onto duck-boarding. The option exists for a short detour from the route, ahead to the causeway bridge and the boathouse beyond it, via former, and still well-defined, salterns. *The walk route takes you right, to follow the course indicated by a low-level path sign as it skirts a field and takes you, via a gate, to the reserve's bird hide (left),* which can be visited and displays the latest information on the many species of bird life here.

Leaving the hide, go right, up a short, climbing path. emerging at the roadside via a gate alongside Marsh Farm House. Bear left along the road for a short distance, then use the stile (left) that provides access to a broad stretch of grass pathway.

No ordinary pathway, this. It used to be Gold Street, Newtown's principal shopping thoroughfare. Butchers and bakers, weavers and tailors – and more than one of them in most cases – plied their trade in the town centuries ago and Gold Street would certainly have accommodated a good many of them. Was the blacksmith here as well? And the tavern? It's all long since returned to nature.

Not all of Gold Street has disappeared. *A stile at the path's far end takes you to a corner of the road linking Newtown with neighbouring Porchfield* – Gold Street's continuation. You get a much better impression of old Newtown's former dimensions when you look down the full length of this virtually straight section of road. The town may have declined in size and population following its 14th century hammering, but that long road ahead was once confined entirely within Newtown's precincts. *Carry on, straight ahead, to join the road – it's usually quiet – and stay with it all the way to, and just beyond, a sharp right-hand bend. Look out for the stile (right) (C) at the start of footpath CB13a, signposted back to Newtown.* In centuries past, this area was known as Town Gate, although the precise location of the former gateway itself is uncertain.

Having crossed the stile, walk straight ahead, following the waymarked route through gaps in two hedges and over a stile before bearing right, then left, to reach another stile at a location recorded on 18th century maps as Bowling Green. Whether bowls was actually played here is a matter for fascinating conjecture. *Ahead of you is a hedge-lined, grass-surfaced track.* This is – or was – the eastern section of the old town's High Street, an *image somewhat easier to conjure up after the track emerges, via a swing gate, at the former crossroads*, with the surviving part of High Street straight ahead. *Go left,* passing the National Trust-owned building that was once the Newtown Arms (note the old town crest affixed to the front wall). Also recalled as the Noah's Ark, this remained the local pub until last orders were finally called in 1916.

Walk a few paces further. You have now arrived at the romantically incongruous location of the Old Town Hall (D). Yes, Newtown, totally devoid of shops and possessing only a pub with no beer, does still have a functioning town hall! Amazingly, despite the modest and declining state of its fortunes, in 1584 the town not only retained the right to municipal government but was actually declared a Parliamentary borough by Elizabeth I. For the next 250 years, Newtown's small and dwindling band of townsmen elected not one, but two MPs to represent their interests. From 1699, the probable date of the town hall's construction, they had a building worthy of this exalted status. The town hall was funded by public subscription – in a town that had boasted just 15 inhabited buildings in 1636.

It was an easy route to Parliament for many. Newtown's MPs included John Churchill, the first Duke of Marlborough (1768), and George Canning (1804), who became Foreign Secretary and Prime Minister. It is safe to assume that neither would have needed to devote much time to constituency matters!

Newtown was a classic 'rotten borough' and was ripe for the picking when the first Reform Act stripped it of its Parliamentary representation in 1832. Soon afterwards, the Corporation itself was wound up, a Government Commission commenting it was "not probable that there is an inhabitant capable of exercising any municipal function." Following a period as a school, then a private house, the town hall was reduced to an ivy-clad ruin before it was spectacularly rescued and presented to the National Trust by a colourful band of anonymous benefactors, collectively known as Ferguson's Gang, in 1933.

Today, Calbourne Parish Council, within whose boundaries Newtown now falls, continues to use the town hall as a meeting chamber, thus preserving something of the use the building was originally provided for. This extraordinary relic of former importance is open to the public on certain days. Newtown itself is open at all times. It no longer fears invasion from abroad. On the contrary, it does all it can to embrace it, though these days the foreign invaders come by air rather than sea. Waders, ducks, geese. Some breed here; others flock to Newtown's estuary – a nature reserve since 1966 – to escape the Arctic winter. It's the birds who benefit the most today from the 'free town.'

Leave Newtown by carrying on in the same direction, downhill, back to the bridge. Then use in reverse the route taken earlier all the way back to the New Inn at Shalfleet.

Shalfleet's Church of St Michael the Archangel incorporates elements of the original 11th century church. The squat tower is the most obvious example. Its walls are more than five feet thick and, until 1889, it had no external entrance, evidence of its use in former days as a place of refuge for villagers in the event of enemy raids on the nearby coast. The church was capable of hitting back, too. For a long time, up until the late-18th century, a 3-pounder gun was kept at the base of the tower.

Cross the main road with caution and continue straight ahead into Church Lane, which bends right after a short distance to skirt the churchyard boundary. Look out for a stile (left) at the start of a signposted footpath to Newbridge (the S17 – though it's not designated as such on the direction sign). *Its route takes you past a pleasant open area (seating), then bears left to a stile and, immediately beyond it, a planked bridge across a stream.*

Continue between a hedge and small trees to reach another stile (left), then bear slightly right and head for yet another, alongside a stream, soon followed by the fifth stile on the footpath. Continue in the same direction at the foot of a sloping field, bordered by trees and hedges (left), to reach a planked bridge and the sixth stile. The seventh and eighth, separated by another stream bridge, follow at the next field boundary, and the ninth, straight ahead, takes you from the far side of the field beyond it along a diagonal, climbing route to the right, crossing a field to the tenth stile, alongside a farm gate.

The footpath directional sign at this point confirms that you are walking a section of the Hamstead Trail. Follow its route ahead, bearing slightly left, with the path now bordered on the right by fencing, to reach a stile and gate. Use either to follow the signposted route to Newbridge along a track-lane (often muddy) which takes you through a farmyard (Homestead Farm). Leave the lane as it bends left, down a slope, and carry on straight ahead to a stile, now on signposted footpath S35.

Follow the trodden route beyond the stile to reach another, providing access to the roadside (E). Newbridge village centre is up the road on the right. Your route takes you left, down the road for a short distance, to a junction. Turn right here and walk up the hill as far as a sharp left-hand bend. Look out at this point for a stile directly ahead, the start of footpath CB11, signposted to Calbourne Mill. The descending path bears right to reach a path junction. Take the waymarked route to the right. It leads you down steps and across a stream bridge, then bends sharp left to run through a small area of woodland before rising into a field. The climb initially continues, then the field path descends and bends right to a path junction at Eades Farm.

Go left here, using a stile to follow the designated route of footpath S23, signposted to Dodpitts Lane, through a field, a route bordered initially by a hedge (left). After negotiating a pair of stiles, separated by a planked stream bridge, continue in the same direction through the field beyond to reach another stile and bridge combination (left). The path then enters a section of Chessell Copse (often muddy in places), taking you to a further stile, before following a meandering, rising route to emerge from the copse at yet another stile. Bear left, following the waymarked, climbing route through a field to a metal gate at the side of Dodpitts Lane (where the footpath sign pointing back to Newbridge serves as a locational aid as you approach the road).

Cross the road and go left for a few paces to join footpath S34, signposted to Churchill Farm and Broad Lane, on your right, initially a broad pathway between fields. Stay with it onto a rough, and then grassy, surface, ignoring all turns-off, as the route takes you to a stile, marked by a white path indicator disc on a post. Follow the trodden route sharp right immediately beyond the stile and descend the slope to a second indicator disc. Bear left here across a field, making for an indicator post with two discs. Take the route to the right, still crossing the field, and make for the next white disc, visible ahead. Go past it, straight ahead and down the slope, to reach the final disc on this section of route, alongside a footpath directional sign.

Emerging at the side of a lane (Wellow Top Road – F on the map), opposite Alma Cottage, cross over and go left along this quiet country lane. It takes you down a short hill, past farm buildings, cottages and a stream, then up and on to the post office serving Wellow village. A few paces further bring you to a junction with the B3401. Cross it with care and bear left. (For those doing the walk in shorter stages, you are now on the route of the 7A bus service for Yarmouth.)

Continuing the walk, carry on on alongside the road, taking care where there is no pavement, to pass through Wellow and, half-a-mile further on, enter Thorley village. Soon after passing the distinctive village church, cross the road and go left, up another quiet rural byway. Keeping to the side of the road on the right, climb as far as the footpath sign denoting the start of path Y1 to Yarmouth (right).

The well-defined path runs between fencing (left) and hedge, then rises and falls before skirting a wildlife management area (left) and, later, crossing a minor road (the continuation on the far side of the road is slightly to the right, up a small bank).

With the signpost pointing in the direction of Millers Copse, continue straight ahead until the path turns sharply to the left, and then to the right, to run alongside small trees (left). Follow the path's meandering route until it climbs eventually to reach the access point to the copse (left). On entering, follow the main pathway straight ahead through the copse, a conservation area managed by the Wight Nature Fund. The path onwards is easy to follow as it takes you, via metal gates, to its junction with the signposted Y19 bridleway – along the formation of the old Freshwater, Yarmouth & Newport Railway.

Turn right onto the track and walk the short distance to Yarmouth's former station, which has changed little since the line's closure in 1953 and now serves as the town's youth centre. Leave the bridleway route via the platform exit (left), then walk up Station Road, staying with it round a left-hand bend, then turning right into Mill Lane, which provides access to the main road straight ahead. Cross the road carefully and continue in the same direction along St James's Street to reach the town centre and finish point.

Seeking out the Tudor cows in the old port of Shamblord

This short walk of just under 5 miles (8km) links the sites of the Tudor forts at East and West Cowes. The outward leg follows the direct route along the coastline, running through the centres of the twin towns either side of the River Medina and crossing the river via the floating bridge. The return leg adopts an inland route through Northwood Park and the southern outskirts of (West) Cowes before returning you to the bridge and the finish point at East Cowes. The only appreciable climbing involved is immediately beyond the parkland, up Park Road. There are no stiles on the walk, which is mainly on street pavements, but also includes some footpaths.

Introduction: Why Cowes? It's a name synonymous the world over with sailing. The most famous place-name on the Isle of Wight. It's always been Cowes, hasn't it? Actually, it hasn't. In the beginning there was Shamblord, newly developed as a haven at the mouth of the River Medina when the recognised trading ports of Wight were reduced to three – Eremue (Yarmouth) in the west, Shamblord at the northern tip and La Riche (Ryde) in the east – by 14th century decree. This was done to restrict movement to and from the Island as a security measure against the frequent attacks by French raiders.

Henry VIII was inspired by the same motive two centuries later when he ordered the construction of a string of fortifications to defend The Solent and its coastline. To protect the river mouth at Shamblord, two forts were built either side of it in 1539, using stone from the recently-suppressed abbeys of Quarr, on the Island, and Beaulieu, on the mainland. They were called the East and West Cows.

Parking and Public Transport: There are main road connections to East Cowes from Ryde and Newport. Direct access from Cowes, across the River Medina, is provided by the famous floating bridge (free for pedestrians). The start of the walk at Old Castle Point is a short distance from East Cowes seafront's public car park. Frequent

Southern Vectis bus services link East Cowes with Ryde (route 4) and Newport (routes 5 and 37). Nearest bus stops are in Castle Road and the Red Funnel ferry terminal – the proximity of which makes this an easy walk for day trippers Tudor Southampton.

Information: As the whole route of the walk lies within the towns on either side of the Medina, there is no shortage of toilet or refreshment facilities – inevitably the choice is expanded during the summer months – and plenty of opportunities to take a rest on one of the many seats provided, particularly along the seafronts and within Northwood Park. The floating bridge runs at frequent intervals.

Directions:
Old Castle Point (A on the map) is at the far end of East Cowes Esplanade – literally. Before setting off, three points of clarification. First, while the 'old castle' is assumed to refer to Henry VIII's original East Cow, it is by no means certain that the Tudor fort actually stood on this point. It seems logical, yet there is a theory that, because subsequent land reclamation has extended the coastline to the north, Henry's fort may have occupied a site rather more inland today – a feasible suggestion. Second, the present castellated structure at the point has nothing whatsoever to do with Tudor fortifications; and third, neither has the East Cowes Castle built for his principal Isle of Wight home by the great Regency architect John Nash. It has long been accepted that no trace remains today of Henry VIII's East Cow.

Leaving the point (grid ref SZ 511965 – marked A on the route map), walk westwards along the Esplanade towards the town centre.

The view across Cowes Harbour is always full of interest. Naturally, this is especially so in the sailing season, and particularly during Cowes Week in August, when the global yachting fraternity descend *en masse* on the twin towns at the mouth of the Medina, transforming the atmosphere into a cosmopolitan carnival.

Sailing as a sport was still a thing of the future, of course, when Henry VIII first took an interest in Shamblord. Were the castles named after the cow-like features of a sandbank which lay off the coast? The shifting sands of time have obscured their precise origin, but the name has stuck ever since.

East Cowes can point to a rich post-Tudor history, built on the

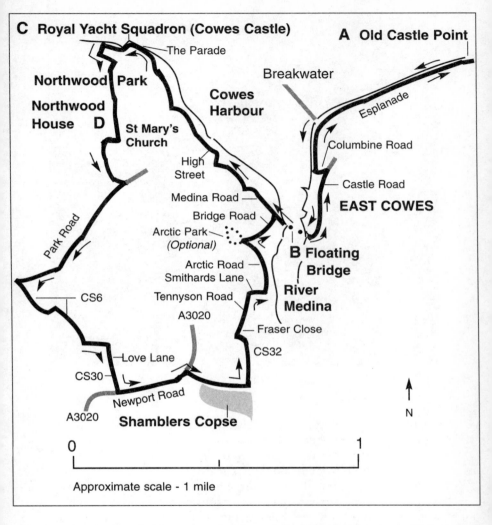

C **Royal Yacht Squadron (Cowes Castle)**   A **Old Castle Point**

The Parade

Northwood Park   Breakwater

Cowes Harbour

Northwood House   **D**   Esplanade

St Mary's Church   Columbine Road

High Street   Castle Road

Medina Road   **EAST COWES**

Bridge Road

Arctic Park *(Optional)*   B **Floating Bridge**

Arctic Road   **River Medina**

Smithards Lane

Tennyson Road

A3020   Fraser Close

CS6   CS32

Love Lane

CS30

Park Road

A3020   Newport Road   N

Shamblers Copse

0   1

Approximate scale - 1 mile

twin planks of ship construction and the Royal Patronage of the Victorian era. Reminders of both abound on this opening stretch of the walk.

After passing East Cowes Sailing Club's dinghy park and the adjoining car park – just before the Cambridge Road junction (left) – look out for a striking reminder of the area's shipbuilding heritage. HMS *Cavalier*, built in Cowes in 1944 by J. Samuel White's, is the last remaining Second World War Royal Navy

John Nash's East Cowes Castle – an engraving from the early-19th century of the successor to Henry VIII's tudor fort. Neither has survived.

destroyer. Sadly for the Island, she is today berthed in Chatham Historic Dockyard, but at least her propeller is here – a gift from Southern Water after its completion of drainage works in 1994.

Information plaques along the seafront record not only the story of *Cavalier*, but also that of the historic buildings which have brought so much character and tradition to the East Cowes waterfront over the years. Look for the old coastguard station and its cottages (built in 1881 and handed over to the local council in 1924) and the site of Victoria Barracks (opened in 1872 and home for a detachment of the Brigade of Guards during spells of guard duty up the hill at Osborne, the house and estate acquired in 1845 by the Queen and Prince Consort for redevelopment as a country retreat).

Then, as you *bear left at the end of the Esplanade, (toilets, right)* there is Columbine Works, from whose giant shed Saunders-

Roe proudly introduced the world to Christopher Cockerell's hovercraft in 1959. Was it a ship or was it a plane? In fact. the hovercraft was a cross between the two, a neat metaphor for the manufacturing traditions of Saunders-Roe itself, a 1928 collaboration between boatbuilders S. E. Saunders and the aircraft manufacturing company, A. V. Roe. Amphibious machines had long been a speciality – a prodigious number of seaplanes for Britain's war effort and huge commercial flying boats for passenger use – so the hovercraft was something of a natural progression. A string of bigger and better hovercraft rolled off the production line to follow the pioneering SR.N1, but, while they all carried the proud distinguishing initials, the company had been swallowed up as part of Westlands and then became part of the British Hovercraft Corporation. Now, what's left of the business in East Cowes is operated as part of GKN Aerospace Services.

The left turn takes you into Columbine Road. Follow it for a short distance before turning right into Castle Street. Carry on along it, noting just before the crossroads the re-use by Saunders-Roe (and now GKN) of the town's former Kings Cinema (left). *Go straight ahead at the crossroads/mini-roundabout (there is a pedestrian crossing up the road to the left) and walk past the car parks for Red Funnel and Trinity House (right) as you follow the road's left bend to reach the floating bridge (B).* The sight of a distinctively red lightship in port for maintenance, so long a feature of Cowes Harbour, will soon be a thing of the past, when Trinity House moves the operation to its Harwich depot in Essex. Trinity Pier's most noted departure was the body of Queen Victoria, following her death at Osborne in 1901.

Floating bridges – or chain ferries – were provided where the lie of the land made a fixed bridge impossible. The banks of the Medina were finally linked by the chains in 1859, thus eliminating the need for a lengthy road journey via Newport, and a succession of floating bridges have clanked their way across the river ever since, taking just a few minutes, but always giving way to sail.

Leaving the floating bridge on the west bank, walk straight ahead along Medina Road towards Cowes town centre.

Development at the port of Shamblord began in earnest during the 13th century but seems to have been confined largely to the east bank. Given the geographical location, the adequate depth of available water and an abundance of accessible oak trees from which to cut the frames and timbers for Henry VIII's fleet, shipbuilding was a logical progression in Tudor times. Demand for Cowes-built ships grew steadily over the next 200 years. From the late 18th century, substantial men-o'-war were being turned out for the Royal Navy in the former Nye yard on the Medina. Boats, as well as ships, were constructed, notably the Cowes ketch, mass-produced throughout the 19th century and widely employed as a versatile workboat. The harbour, meanwhile, developed international seaborne trade, watched over by the Customs House at East Cowes, engaged from the start in a constant battle with the smugglers whose activities have plagued the Isle of Wight for centuries.

Considerably more welcome was the shipbuilder Thomas White, who acquired the old Nye yard in 1803 and moved his already long-established family business to Cowes from Broadstairs, Kent. White's thereafter expanded to become the most illustrious shipbuilding dynasty Cowes has ever known.

It lasted for 160 years, most notably under the ownership of Thomas's grandson, John Samuel. The company's ships had a much-envied reputation for quality, whether the production line was turning out cross-Channel steamers or warships for naval fleets worldwide. Into the latter category fell the destroyer *Blyskavica*, built for the Polish Navy just before the Second World War. Back at Cowes for a refit in May 1942, her guns blazed away at the Luftwaffe during a particularly vicious onslaught on the port. Recalled locally as the Cowes Blitz, this was the single most devastating air raid of the Island's eventful war. It is widely acknowledged that the presence of the *Blyskavica* saved Cowes from total annihilation on that terrible night. Happily, the ship survives, preserved in Poland.

It was a sad day indeed for the Isle of Wight when J. Samuel White's closed down in 1965. Much of its former infrastructure survives in different guise along, and just off, Medina Road, but the great days of shipbuilding at Cowes died with its closure. Happily, other famous Cowes firms allied to the maritime trades are still with us in more than mere name, fed by the incessant demand for yachting paraphernalia. Medina Road is book-ended by sailmakers Ratsey & Lapthorn and the Clare Lallow yard.

Continue in the same direction as road and pavement rise to join Birmingham Road (with the town's police station on the left), then carry on ahead into the High Street.

The famously narrow shopping thoroughfare, which annually bulges at the seams during regatta week in August, is geared heavily to the yachting trade. Its route takes you from the present marina entrance (right), via Red Funnel's Fountain Pier (terminal for the fast passenger-only Red Jets to Southampton), and, further along (right), the Sir Max Aitken Maritime Museum, housed in the old Prospect sail-loft and a mecca for sailing historians.

Having walked the full length of High Street, ignoring all turns-off, carry on through Bath Road to emerge on the seafront (public toilets, right) at The Parade. Though devoid since 1961 of its pier, The Parade remains a popular promenade, especially during Cowes Week's yachting extravaganza. *Bear left and walk the short distance along to the headquarters of the Royal Yacht Squadron (C) –* reputedly the world's most exclusive club.

Fittingly, the building that houses the Squadron was put there by Royal command, for this is Cowes Castle – Henry VIII's West Cow. The old Tudor fort, of course, would have looked nothing like it does today – and nothing like it did when a group of aristocrats and gentlemen met in London to form The Yacht Club in 1813. Their principal motive seems to have been a need to counter the take-over of London society – and its clubs – by Beau Brummel and the Dandies. The acquisition of the Royal prefix added further sheen to the exclusivity of the new club, which in 1825 set up home in the Isle of Wight, eight years later restyling itself as the Royal Yacht Squadron. In 1866 it re-located from elsewhere in the town to the premises it has occupied ever since at Cowes Castle, then serving as the official residence of the Governor of the Isle of Wight.

Modifications in the 17th and 18th centuries had left little more than the gun platform surviving from the Tudor fort. Cannons still fire from it today, signalling the start of the Cowes Week racing. If you're walking this route during the regatta week, it's advisable to take heed of the warning notices!

With the establishment of the Royal Yacht Squadron at the castle, and the social status that flowed inevitably from it, West Cowes assumed major prominence. Its subsequent development outstripped that of East Cowes across the river. The 'West' prefix was formally abandoned. This *was* Cowes.

Bear right to walk round the frontage of the castle, beside the sea, and its grounds beyond, before turning left and uphill for a short distance to reach Queens Road. Go left here, passing Holy Trinity Church (right), then turn right and climb the short distance into Castle Road and, directly opposite, the steps leading to Northwood Park. Use the impressive entrance to enter the park (D),

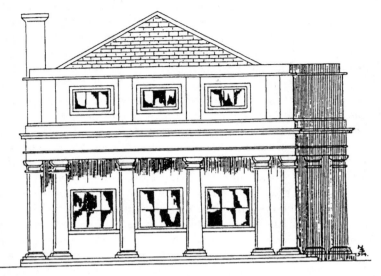

A drawing by John Nash for one of the two lodges built for George Ward at Northwood House.

continuing straight ahead up the pathway beyond the steps.

As information panels dotted around the park explain, the old manor of Northwood was acquired in 1801 by George Ward and, following further land purchase and extensive landscaping, it was known as Northwood Park by 1817. Private ownership ended in 1929 when the estate was bequeathed to Cowes Urban District Council. Though the development of post-war housing has substantially shrunk the original dimensions, it remains a spacious area of parkland, now in the care of the Isle of Wight Council. The old estate's boundary wall, running the length of Baring Road, provides a good example of traditional Isle of Wight coursing in Bembridge limestone quarried at nearby Gurnard.

Stay with the path as it passes to the left of Northwood House (D), added by George Ward's son in 1823 and bearing the hallmarks of a John Nash design – though it was not finished until three years after the great architect's death. With St Mary's Church (plain West Cowes Chapel when it was built during the 17th century Protectorate) coming up on the left, *go right, up a section of path alongside the house's southern perimeter. Bear left with this path to reach a four-way path junction.* A very short detour to the right will provide access to the remains of Northwood's ice house (look for the explanatory panel, then pass through a gap in the hedge to the domed roof which protrudes above ground). The use of ice houses in England dates back to the Tudor period – the best Island example is preserved at Osborne.

Returning from the ice house to the path junction, go right, down a route between hedgerows, to emerge at a car park. Turn left to follow the designated walkway down the side of the car park to reach Park Road. Cross to the far side of the road and go right, uphill, ignoring all turns-off as far as a recreation ground, immediately beyond the limit of housing. Turn left here to follow the route of footpath CS6 (signposted to Love Lane).

The sloping path takes you alongside playing fields (right) before dividing near a modern housing development. Take its left-hand fork here and follow the winding route between the new houses, across an estate road and along a final section on new pathway to emerge in Love Lane. Go right here, alongside the road. continuing straight on when it converts to footpath status and takes you to the edge of the A3054 Newport Road. Go left and, when it is safe to do so, cross to the far side of the road, then continue past Northwood Cemetery before turning right, down the approach to Arctic Road and the signposted cycleway. The woodland ahead of you, on the right, is a rare reminder of old Shamblord, recalled in its name – Shamblers Copse.

Opposite the cycleway access point (right) near the foot of the approach road, go left to join a footpath (CS32) that climbs to reach the track of the old rail line from Newport, then runs between new housing. At the end of the footpath, go left, up a tarmac-surfaced path, to the roadside (Fraser Close). Turn right and carry on in the same direction into Tennyson Road, before turning right down Smithards Lane. Near the bottom was the location of the last operational level crossing on the Island, where the gates, contrary to common practice, were kept closed across the road until the occasional vehicle using it demanded their opening!

At the foot of Smithards Lane, turn left into Arctic Road and follow its route as it climbs to a three-way junction with Bernard Road (ahead) and Bridge Road (right). Either go right into Bridge Road or, to add further interest and only a few minutes to the walk, go left through wooden barriers into what is now known as Arctic Park but functioned until railway closure in February 1966 as Mill Hill's station. The platform face and the tunnel beneath Cowes, immediately beyond it, are clearly evident to the right.

Leave this small park by the path rising to the road on the far side, then turn right, and right again, across the mouth of the tunnel, to rejoin Arctic Road. Take the turn (now left) down Bridge Road. It returns you to Medina Road. Go right at the junction, walk the short distance to the floating bridge and retrace your steps in East Cowes back to the Esplanade start point.

The 18th century scandal that marked the end for the Island's great houses

You need a full day to undertake this 12-mile (19.2km) walk linking the two great houses that dominated Isle of Wight society in the 18th century until they were rocked by a sensational scandal. Although long, the walk involves no steep climbs as it threads its way through the mainly flat arable land of East Wight. The route combines sections of peaceful rural pathways with easy walking stretches along parts of the Newport-Sandown cycleway (mostly on the former rail line) and along quiet country lanes. There are a number of stiles to negotiate, but the route is well-defined for most of the way and you may well find the only other obstacle is opening the heavy wrought iron gateway, near the start and finish, at Appuldurcombe's extraordinary triumphal arch!

Introduction: Eighteenth century society on the Isle of Wight revolved around the mansions at Appuldurcombe and Knighton Gorge. The origins of both houses extend much further back into history, but they were in their heyday when the amorous escapades of the notorious Lady Seymour Worsley contrived to set them on a simultaneous path to ignominious decline. It ended in ruin for Appuldurcombe and obliteration for Knighton Gorges. The former is open to the public in a partially restored state. At Knighton, all that is left is the mound on which the palatial mansion once stood, the house's gateposts – and the ghosts of the past.

Parking and Public Transport: Wroxall lies on the B3327, north-west of Ventnor and a short distance south of the A3020 Newport-Shanklin route at Whiteley Bank crossroads. Parking is available at the start of the walk, off St Martin's Road in the centre of the village (reached from the B3320 via Station Road). Wroxall is on the routes of Southern Vectis buses between Cowes (except Sundays), Newport and Ventnor (services 3 and 3A), Ryde, Sandown, Shanklin and Ventnor (services 7 and 7A) and the local circular service 31 from St Lawrence and Ventnor (Sundays excepted). The village's principal bus stops are located at Wroxall Church, near the walk's start point.

Information: There is a range of village facilities (shops, public toilets and The Worsley pub) at Wroxall. Facilities on a smaller scale (including The Pointer Inn) exist near the walk's midway point at Newchurch. South of Newchurch, there is easy access to both the Fighting Cocks Inn and the nearby Amazon World Zoo Park, but the bulk of the route is in open countryside, devoid of facilities.

Directions:
Begin the walk at the St Martin's Road car park (grid ref SZ 552797 – marked A on the route map). This area of Wroxall was redeveloped following the controversial closure of the Shanklin-Ventnor rail link in April 1966, just a few months short of the centenary of its opening at the height of Victorian railway expansion. Traces of the former station are evident as you begin the walk by going *left from the car park towards the village centre.* Immediately before making the left turn into Station Road, look directly ahead to what used to be Wroxall Hotel, where a refreshment room once opened onto the station platform. *Walk the short distance down Station Road to join the High Street, with The Worsley pub opposite.*

Turn right to walk past St John the Evangelist Church (toilets opposite) and the Castle Road junction, then go down the hill on the raised pavement, before crossing the road and continuing the descent past Avenue Road to take the next left-hand turn into Appuldurcombe Road (signposted to Appuldurcombe House / Park and the Isle of Wight Owl & Falconry Centre). Walk down the hill, ignoring all turns-off, then climb this increasingly rural route, with Stenbury Down as its backdrop, past the caravan park entrance and beyond a road junction (right), following the directional sign for bridleway GL44. Immediately after the start of the designated access route to Appuldurcombe House (the entrance to which is further up the hill), use the stepped stile on the right onto the bridleway (signposted to Godshill).

Appuldurcombe's origins as a manor date back to 1102, when it was presented by Richard de Redvers, Norman Lord of the Island, to the Benedictine abbey he had founded in Normandy. Sir Robert Worsley began the present house early in the 18th century, and it was finished towards the end of the century by a descendant,

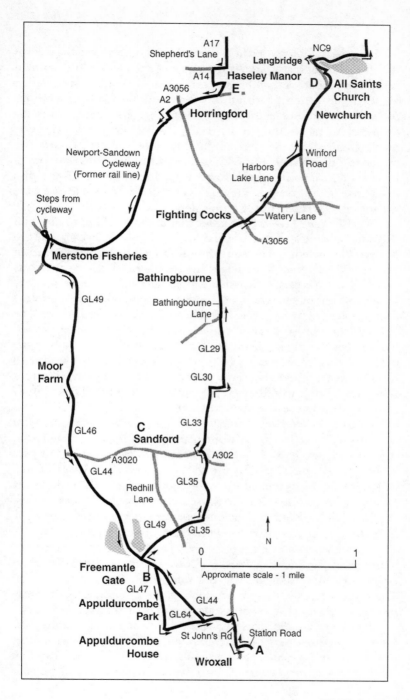

Sir Richard Worsley – army officer, MP, Governor of the Isle of Wight and local historian. As the home of the Island's pre-eminent gentleman, Appuldurcombe was a magnet for English society life. Sir Richard's penchant for all things beautiful – fed by a fabulous collection of 'treasures' from his extensive travels – extended to the choice of his wife – and led to scandal. Lady Seymour Worsley was much admired for her extraordinarily good looks. Admired by rather too many, as it turned out. Her many extra-marital affairs included a serious fling with Captain George Maurice Bisset, who lived at Knighton Gorges. Eloping to London in 1781, the two were caught in bed together at Westminster,

Worlsey sued Bisset, his former friend, for "making assault" on Seymour when the scandal of the lovers' discovery became all too common knowledge. The court found in his favour, but instead of the £20,000 claimed in damages by the Island's Governor, he was awarded just sixpence! Worsley was judged by the court to have known all about his wife's wild sexual adventures – she admitted during evidence to 23 lovers – and had even encouraged them. The fall-out from this scandalous episode was immense. Worlsey retired from public life, dying in 1805. Appuldurcombe's glory days at the centre of everything were numbered and Bisset, though he had to fork out just a few pence as the price for his indiscretion, entered a slow decline that would eventually lead to the total destruction of his own great house at Knighton Gorges.

Part of the Worsley Trail, the well-defined path cuts across a field, through delightful pastoral scenery, to reach a metal gate. Beyond it, the route rises to pass between two trees to a second gate at a pathway junction. Ignoring the route (right) to Redhill Lane, stay with GL44 as it meanders through the foothills of Stenbury Down and rises towards what must surely rank as one of the most extraordinary features you will encounter on a country path – the Ionic triumphal arch at Freemantle Gate (B on the map).

Freemantle was the principal gateway to the northern boundary of Sir Richard Worsley's 18th century landscaped park at Appuldurcombe, designed by the renowned 'Capability' Brown. The great arched gateway bears all the signs of faded magnificence, though its wrought iron gates have been restored in recent years.

Just short of the gate, the route forms a junction with path GL47 (signposted left to Appuldurcombe House). At Freemantle, pass through the smaller gate to the left of the main archway and carry on ahead for a short distance before turning right, through a

Appuldurcombe House – an engraving of the former Worsley mansion during its period of ownership by the Earl of Yarborough in the early-19th century. In 1854 it was sold by auction, ceasing to function as a private residence.

large metal gate, to join bridleway GL49 for the next part of the walk to Redhill Lane.

The path veers right and then runs along a fenced-off field boundary, initially rising, then descending to a wooden gate and continuing between fencing and bushes/trees down a section often muddy after rain to reach another gate. Still descending, the route follows a field boundary, bordered on the right by small trees, to a stile, beyond which it completes its descent down the edge of a further field to emerge, via another wooden gate, at the roadside in Redhill Lane.

Cross the road – there's normally very little traffic – and bear slightly to the left to pass through a metal gate and join bridleway GL35 on its signposted route to Sandford. Initially bordered by a tall hedgerow (left) and fencing, the path descends to a wooden gate, then runs between hedgerow (small trees) and an electrified fence (right), beyond its junction with a waymarked footpath (GL38), before bearing left through a gap in the hedge to a gate. Unless you are taking the short detour to visit the donkey sanctuary (along the well-trodden route to the right), follow the waymarked route straight ahead between wooden posts, keeping the hedged-in field boundary to your left.

The route eventually takes you to a wooden gate (left). Beyond it, continue in the same direction, with a hedge now on your right at the foot of an upwardly sloping field. Passing through a large metal gate, follow the fenced-in farm track beyond it as far as its sharp turn to the right. Go through the metal gate ahead of you at this point and continue in the same direction along a fenced-in section of grass pathway which leads you to another metal gate, immediately before arrival at the side of the A3020, east of Sandford.

Cross the main road with care, then go left along the pavement towards the sharp left-hand bend by the easily identified Sandford Methodist Church (C). Just before the bend, bear right at the access to The Cottage (thatched), then go left to the start of signposted footpath GL33 to Bobblestone, The path bears right to a stile. Follow the waymarked route beyond it, left, across a field, marked for most of the way by an electric fence, right, to reach a double stile in the hedgerow. The route continues along a hedge-lined field boundary, passing a path junction – marked by a double stile on the right – to exit the field via another stile.

Turn right here, down an unmarked track, looking out for steps (left) leading to a stile at the start of footpath GL29, signposted to Bathingbourne. The route of this path, fenced to the right, takes you due north along the side of a field. Immediately before a metal gate, cross the stile to its left, then carry on in the same direction as before to another stile and gate combination. Follow the path as it skirts the hedge-lined field boundary beyond the stile and eventually descends to emerge at a road bend (Bathingbourne Lane).

This quiet country lane offers pleasant walking as the route continues straight ahead. Stay with it, ignoring a footpath junction, as it passes Bathingbourne Farm (right), then crosses a stream at tranquil Bathingbourne Bridge and bends right at a fork in the road to reach its junction with the A3056 at Fighting Cocks Crossroads. Cross this busy road with caution and maintain your direction on the grass verge alongside Watery Lane, the first section of which – as far as the access to Amazon World – carries a significant amount of traffic. It's much less busy beyond the access junction as it continues past Newchurch Sports Pavilion and Hall (right). Leave Watery Lane as it bends sharp right and continue in the same direction as before, along the road straight ahead (Harbors Lake Lane), following the directional sign to Newchurch.

This quiet road rises, then bends right to run past housing to form a 'T' junction with Winford Road. Go left here, initially on *the wide grass verge, then on the opposite side of the road, and follow the traffic-calmed route all the way into Newchurch village centre, passing The Pointer Inn (right) to arrive at All Saints Church (D on the map).*

Newchurch is old. It was one of the Isle of Wight's original six parishes, extending from the Island's north coast to the south and including the present-day towns of Ryde and Ventnor at either end. The 11th century All Saints Church was among the half-dozen donated by William Fitz-Osbern, Norman Lord of the Island, to the abbey of Lyre in Normandy, entitling its monks to collect the tithes and rents from all six. Inside All Saints, the memorial-lined transept served as mortuary chapel for the Dillington family of nearby Knighton Gorges for 200 years. Outside the church, the view from the hilltop church across the peaceful Vale of Newchurch is unrivalled.

Walk the full length of the churchyard (adjacent to the road) to exit via a small metal gate, then go down the steps beyond and follow the descending pathway route through pleasant woodland until it bends right onto a track. Go left here, still descending, following the track between trees to emerge near the roadside (left) at Parsonage Farm. Use the pedestrian area at the side of the road to complete the descent to Langbridge – the 'long bridge' over the River Yar – and the Newport-Sandown cycleway. For most of its route, the cycleway uses the trackbed of the former rail line which connected the towns until closure in 1956. Newchurch's station was here at Langbridge (on the right), where the line crossed the road.

Following the cycleway direction sign for Sandown (footpath route NC9), go right at the white-fenced access point and follow the pathway to join the old railway route/cycleway. Bear left and remain on the cycleway as far as its junction (left) with footpath NC53, signposted to Knighton. Follow this wide track as it rises gradually through open countryside to arrive at a road bend (Lower Knighton Lane). Walk straight ahead as the lane – which carries little traffic – climbs gently to form a junction on a bend with the main route from Newchurch (left).

Using the roadside (the grass verge where available), carry on in the same direction to follow the road as it bends, rises and then dips to reach a junction (right) with the road serving the self-contained, sleepy hamlet of Knighton. Islanders always refer to it as K-nighton to distinguish it from Niton, the Island's southern-most village. Many go past Knighton without knowing it's there.

A short walk uphill brings you to the stone pillars guarding the entrance (right) to Knighton Gorges (E on the map).

One visitor to Knighton Gorges in 1800 called it "by far the most considerable and beautiful of the ancient mansions of the Island." Hyperbole or not, this wondrous Elizabethen manor house was just 21 years' short of total obliteration. The name Knighton Gorges comes not from any geological feature in the area, but from Ralph de Gorges, who inherited Knighton manor in the mid-13th century.

The Dillingtons acquired it in Tudor times, holding it for 150 years until the tragic and mysterious death of the last of the line, Sir Tristram Dillington, in 1721. Some say he took his own life following the deaths, in quick succession, of his wife and four or more children. Others maintain he was a life-long bachelor. That he died at Knighton does not seem in doubt, but did he shoot himself or drown in the house's ornamental pool? Theories abound. One suggests that Knighton's butler led Sir Tristram's stallion, Thunderbolt, with his master's body mounted on its back, into the lake in a bid to cover up the suicide. Even today, his ghost is seen after nightfall, astride Thunderbolt. galloping at speed between the gateposts.

Tragedy struck the house a final blow after the scandalous Worsley trial in 1782. Pre-scandal, Captain Bisset's house guests at Knighton had included Sir Joshua Reynolds, David Garrick and John Wilkes, who, it can be imagined, would have taken particular delight in the orgiastic and ritualistic goings-on at the house's notorious Hellfire Club. Society, polite and impolite, shunned Bisset and Knighton after the trial. His long decline into probable insanity had a dramatic climax.

The most colourful version of events suggests that Bisset's opposition to his daughter Jane's romance with a local clergyman led him to forbid either of them from ever setting foot in the great house again if they were to defy him and marry.

When they did exactly that, he set about making good his threat by moving out of the house into his gardener's cottage – and ordering the stone-by-stone demolition of the mansion. The last bit of that tale is generally accepted as fact; the preceding bit is probably legend. Whatever the truth, palatial Knighton Gorges ceased to exist after 1821.

Cross the road, go left and retrace the route from Knighton Gorges almost as far as the junction with Lower Knighton Lane before turning right, up the signposted route of footpath NC7 (to

Mersley Down and Arreton). Follow the path's route at the foot of a sloping field, with a hedge to the left. Eventually, it bends left to a stile, followed immediately by steps down. Veering to the right, NC7 then adopts a well-trodden downward route through a field before turning left to continue as a wide, hedge-lined grass path until a sharp left bend takes it down, to join a track, which then rises (as footpath NC1) to the roadside. Cross the road and go left, looking out for the signposted route of the NC6 bridleway to Arreton (right), which begins on a climbing gravel track.

After a few paces, following the directional sign, bear right and continue along the side of a field, with a hedge to the left, to reach a fork in the track ahead. Take the right-hand track (effectively, straight ahead), and follow its well-defined route to a metal gate and then between fields all the way to a pathway 'T' junction, marked by a directional sign. Go left here (Shepherd's Lane), following the hedge-lined route past houses (left) to reach the entrance to Haseley Manor (F).

Set on an island of greensand rock in the marshes of the Yar, ancient Haseley (the name derives from the Saxon for hazel-wood) was little more than a crumbling ruin until restoration saved it in the 1970s. Shepherd's Lane, a mile-long, dead straight track from the foot of the downs, was once the main driveway to it.

Immediately before the manor entrance, turn right to go down the access lane for a short distance before taking footpath A14 (left), signposted to River Yar and the cycleway. Bordered by hedge (left) and fence, the path bears left to a planked stream bridge, then runs between fencing (initially on a long wood-planked 'bridge') through the area of Haseley's wildlife ponds to re-join the cycleway. Go right, following the signposted route along the former rail line to the A3056 at Horringford, where the old station can be seen across the road, to the left. Go right, along the pavement, and use the light-controlled crossing to reach the opposite side of the road and the next section of the cycleway (footpath route A2), going off to the left. Initially sharing a tarmac-surfaced lane with motor traffic, the cycleway then bears left and descends to take a winding route – much of it on a raised section of wooden planking – to return to the former rail line.

Turn right. Noting original railway fencing (right), remain on the cycleway all the way to a road overbridge (the only one on this section – G on the map) near Merstone. Walk beneath it, then take the steps (right) which lead to the road itself – a quiet country lane.

Turn right, across the bridge, and follow the lane as it winds past houses and, eventually, Merstone Fisheries (left) to reach a three-way bridleway junction. Leaving the lane, follow the signposted route of bridleway A49 to Godshill round a left bend. The bridleway bends to the left, passing its junction with another path (left), then bears right to follow a signposted course between fields, with the high downs around Wroxall now forming the backdrop. *Rising gradually, it eventually passes between hedges, bends left, then right, and carries on to pass through the farmyard at Moor Farm.*

Carry on straight ahead, following the signposted route to Godshill Park. The route now designated as footpath GL46) takes you up to the side of the A3020 at Godshill. Cross the road with care, go left along the grass verge, then turn right to join the climbing bridleway GL44, signposted to Wroxall, passing to the left of a cattle grid. This is also the access road to Godshill Park House and Farm, which are passed (right and left, respectively) *before the bridleway adopts a rough surface and, after descending for a short distance, rises again between fenced-in fields to the edge of woodland (right) and brings you back to the route of the outward part of the walk route at Freemantle Gate. Beyond it, ignore the path used earlier across the fields and follow instead the signposted route of GL47 to Appuldurcombe House, a rough-surfaced track that climbs and then dips to a stile, alongside a metal gate. Carry on, straight ahead, beyond it, passing the car park for Appuldurcombe (left) before arriving at the entrance to the house itself.*

Sir Richard Worsley's niece, Anne, was the last of the family to own the great house. In 1854 it was sold to become an academy for young gentlemen. After the school's closure in 1884, Appuldurcombe took on the role of a monastery for the Benedictine monks of Solesmes, exiled from France, *en route* to their building the new abbey at Quarr in 1908 (see walk 6). The decaying house's final fall from grace, via its use as a billet for soldiers in the 1914-18 war, culminated in 1943, when it was left a roofless ruin thanks to a parachuted land mine from the Luftwaffe. Since then, partially restored but essentially a hauntingly atmospheric shell of its former self, the Worsley dynasty's magnificent home has become an historic monument in the care of English Heritage.

Go left, down the lane, to the stile giving access to footpath GL44, then retrace the outward route back to Wroxall village centre.

Facing up to French aggression
– Puckpool and the Sea Forts

The options within this short, but historically rewarding, coastal walk of no more than 2 miles (3.2km) mean it can be undertaken by anyone who is mobile, including wheelchair users and people with pushchairs or prams. There are good walking surfaces throughout, with no stiles or potential hazards. If the easier options are taken, the walk route can be completed entirely on the level as it traces what remains of some of the key onshore and offshore military defences that were developed around the Island's north-east coast to guard against the threat of 19th century France.

Introduction: Invasion – or the fear of invasion – by French forces was a recurring feature of Isle of Wight history for centuries. The last time the Island faced up to the possibility of attack from our nearest Continental neighbours was in the 19th century. There was widespread concern, verging on panic, throughout the country at the potential danger posed by France's development of new weaponry and particularly the launching of *La Gloire*, the world's first ironclad warship, in 1859. Britain needed to respond with ironclads of her own and had to ensure they were safe from attack when in harbour.

After a Royal Commission in 1860 looked at the state of Britain's coast defences, plans were made to safeguard naval dockyards with modern fortifications. The security of Portsmouth was the foremost consideration. Town and harbour were surrounded by a ring of new fortresses to guard against enemy attack from land or sea. This included the building of four sea forts in the Eastern Solent to protect the dockyard from sea-borne incursion and the construction of a supporting mortar battery at Puckpool Point on the Isle of Wight's north-east coast to cover the Spithead anchorage.

Parking and Public Transport: The start point for the walk is the car park at Appley Park, Ryde (grid ref SX605924 – marked A on the route map), a short distance by road from the town centre. Drive along the Esplanade, heading east out of town, then bear left immediately before the boating lake and follow the road alongside and then beyond the lake to reach its terminal point at Appley. The car park is a short distance up the hill (right, then left). It is possible to reach the start point by using buses on Southern Vectis routes 8 (Ryde-Seaview) and 12 (Ryde-Bembridge-Sandown) and Wight Bus's weekdays-only service 20 (Ryde-Tesco) as far as St John's Church, then descend Appley Lane to the car park. However, the most direct (and fun) access by public transport is the road train that operates for a large part of the year between Ryde (town and seafront) and Puckpool Park, via Appley. The road train stop at Appley is a short walk from the car park. Alternatively, it can itself be used as the start point for the walk – see below.

Information: There are cafés and public toilets at both Appley and Puckpool (where there is also a nearby pub). Note that some of these facilities operate on a seasonal basis. The walk offers many places to sit *en route*.

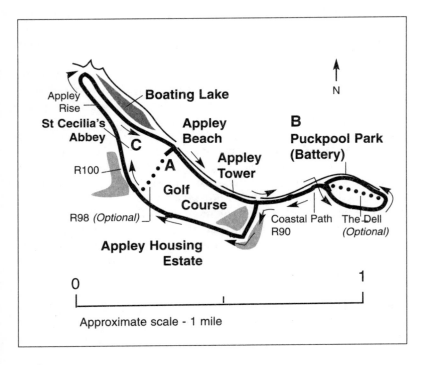

Directions:

The walk begins at the foot of what used to be the Appley estate, sweeping down from the residence at its heart (and not to be confused with the Appley *housing* estate that has for some years occupied the site of the demolished house and its gardens). The erstwhile Ryde Borough Council completed its purchase of the estate in 1945 and subsequently laid it out for the enjoyment of the public.

Leave the car park by turning right and walk the short distance downhill to reach Appley beach (with Ryde Inshore Rescue's headquarters on your left). Take the signposted route of the Coastal Path (right), passing a café (and adjacent road train stop), then public toilets and, finally, a children's playground before arriving at Appley Tower. This walk is concerned mainly with fortifications. Despite its castellated appearance, the tower is very definitely not one of them! It's a Victorian folly, a fanciful addition to the estate by Sir William Hutt, Paymaster-General, during his occupancy of Appley. A folly maybe, but so well established as a dominating part of the seawall 'furniture' that it's hard to imagine this bit of the coastline without it, which is all in stark contrast to Hutt's long vanished private pier.

Historically more significant is the bas-relief commemoration opposite of the ill-fated HMS *Sirius*, principal Naval escort to the 'First Fleet' which sailed from these waters in May 1787 to found modern Australia. *Sirius* arrived there the following January before circumnavigating the globe on a voyage to South Africa to obtain desperately needed provisions for the fledgling colony in New South Wales. It left her in serious need of refurbishment. *Sirius* was careened, repaired and refitted at Mosman Bay, New South Wales, in 1789. Just four months later, sent to Norfolk Island with a mixed load of passsengers and provisions, she ran aground and was wrecked. Two hundred years on, the council in Mosman, NSW, commissioned the commemorative bas-relief for display at Appley, Two others, identical to it, were made at the same time for Mosman Bay itself and Norfolk Island. The dramatic story is set out in full on the plaque accompanying this striking memorial.

So much for ships sailing out. It was, of course, the prospect of them sailing in – uninvited – that led to the construction of the sea forts plonked on three shoals in the Eastern Solent during the 1860s to discourage the French from attacking Portsmouth's dockyard. They're still there, visible from the footpath – Spit Bank (nearest

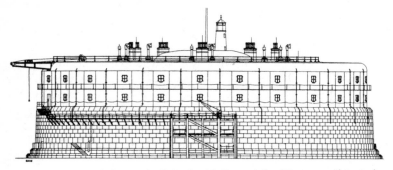

No Man's Land Fort, as built in the 1860s to defend Portsmouth's vital dockyard against the French aggressors. Along with the forts at Spit Bank, Horse Sand and St Helen's, it remains a prominent feature of the eastern Solent – six decades after it ceased to have any military value. The illustration by Garry Mitchell was produced for a series of detailed studies on the coastal fortifications in the Solent area.

Portsmouth), No Man's Land (nearest Ryde) and Horse Sand (roughly in the middle). The trio became a quartet with the addition of St Helens Fort, out of sight around the corner of the coast. The forts had to wait a long time before they were finally able to train their guns on the French. It didn't happen until 1940, in the immediate aftermath of France's collapse in the face of Nazi *blitzkrieg* and the British Government's subsequent decision to immobilize the French fleet. Several of France's warships had escaped from their own Channel ports to seek sanctuary in the Solent – and then found themselves in the firing line of the old forts. In the event, the French ships were taken without the need for the forts to open fire. As the fleet included the battleship *Courbet*. it was just as well. The sea forts. equipped with antiquated weaponry, wouldn't have stood a chance had the battleship fired back!

Two years later, in 1942, the forts' military uselessness was underlined with their downgrading to 'care and maintenance' status, a preliminary step to complete de-actification when the war was over. What to do with them? Their massive construction ruled out demolition so, in 1963, the forts were put up for sale. Not until the 1980s was any real interest shown in acquiring one of them. Spit Bank Fort was bought, restored and opened to the public, via a launch service from the mainland. Since then, the forts at both No Man's Land and Horse Sand have also entered private ownership, with some extraordinary ideas for future use ("luxury jumbo

Horse Sand Fort in 1940 – the year its weaponry was finally trained – but never actually used – against a French warship. Along with the other Spithead forts, Horse Sand was completely de-activated after the war, its military career at an end. Another of Garry Mitchell's superb drawings of the Solent's coastal fortifications.

apartments, complete with butler service," according to the local press, reporting on the latest plans for Horse Sand Fort). Only St Helens Fort remains derelict. Once a year, the tide allows a procession of people to reach it on foot.

Continuing the walk from the tower, the next road train stop is soon reached. A short distance beyond it, leave the path as it curves and climbs to the right, taking instead the ramp down to the sea wall (left). Bear right and continue for a short distance along the sea wall to reach Puckpool Park (B). Leaving the sea wall, turn right immediately before a café (The Pantry) ahead to enter the former battery via the roadway that climbs and then quickly descends, initially to a parking area. Exercising caution, cross the car park to the left side. There are optional routes ahead through the park.

Under the original plan of 1860 for defending Portsmouth and the Spithead anchorage, ten-gun batteries were proposed, in addition to the sea forts, at both Appley House and on Nettlestone Point. A year later the plans were amended in favour of a battery between the two – here at Puckpool. It was built between 1863 and 1865, a battery of 21 mortars in seven groups of three. The combination of a wide ditch and a clay-built, turf-covered rampart provided protection from the sea. Light guns were trained on the adjacent beaches. It wasn't long before the whole layout was changed – in 1867 – in favour of 38 mortars in two rows, with five guns to cover the flanking beaches.

And then, in 1873, it was all change again. Out went eight of the mortars to be replaced by half as many, but more powerful, 11-inch rifled muzzle-loader (RML) guns, two on either flank. The remaining mortars were removed in 1888 and, a year later, in came two more (10.4-inch) RMLs. These two were the most interesting of all the weaponry with which Puckpool was equipped. They were installed in new emplacements, at the centre and the right of the battery, and were built to fire over a concrete parapet rather than through a gap cut for the purpose. The guns were prototypes for the 100-ton Armstrong RMLs later installed in both Gibralter and Malta.

Puckpool's armament was upgraded yet again at the beginning of the 20th century with four breech-loaders (BLs). Two 9.2-inch guns were charged with blasting any battleship attempting an attack on the dockyard, while enemy cruisers and blockships were the intended target for a couple of 6-inchers. That was the theory. The practice was never tested. It took the military authorities until 1908 to acknowledge that the guns were just too far away to offer any effective threat. The smaller pair were transferred to Spit Bank Fort and one of the larger BLs was relegated to reserve status. With removal of the final gun in 1927, Puckpool's life as a military establishment seemed over.

A year later it was sold to the local authority, St Helens Urban District Council. who wasted little time in re-opening it as a public park in 1929. But it wasn't quite the end for military Puckpool. In 1939, together with the holiday camp behind, it officially became a ship! HMS *Medina*, its Second World War designation, was actually a shore base used until 1942 for training men of the Fleet Air Arm and, after that, as Naval accommodation. With hostilities at an end, Puckpool became a public park again – and has remained so.

To explore the remains of the old battery, *either climb onto the former rampart for a high-level perspective or use the path at ground level that runs between the former military buildings (left) and a grass bank.* Two of the early mortar bays survive, near either end of the battery, together with two of the larger RML emplacements (the first seen as you move eastwards across the grass rampart), one of the protected bays for the experimental 10.4-inch RMLs (at the far end) and emplacements for the four later BL guns (in the centre). The protective ditch is seen on the opposite side of the bank. *Return to ground level via the steps leading to a second car park, opposite the crazy golf and play area.*

If the low-level option is chosen, stay with the path, below the gun emplacements as it bears slightly to the left, with a high wall on the right (originally an armaments store for the mortars; later the battery command post for the larger BL guns). *The path emerges into the car park opposite the play area (right). From the car park, take the central roadway left, passing successively on your right public toilets, tennis courts, a bowling green and, finally, a café* (in the battery's former barracks block) *and tea gardens to reach the park's eastern boundary,* site of the battery's original main entrance.

You may be tempted by a quick detour (via a right turn immediately before the café) to visit Puckpool's Wireless Museum. Accommodated in what used to be the battery's married quarters, it's staffed by volunteers and there's no entry fee. Opening times are usually restricted to between 2pm and 4pm on Saturdays and Sundays only.

Back on the park's eastern boundary, turn left up a short slope and begin the return leg of the walk by taking one of two optional routes to the left. Either use the low-level gravel path through The Dell (formerly the battery's protective ditch) *or stay on the tarmac-surfaced path as it bears left and runs along the park's northern boundary, just above the sea wall. Both routes return you to The Pantry café* (but note that the path through The Dell ends with a short climb onto the roadway used when entering the park – the café is then a few paces to the right).

Leave the park and retrace your outward route along the sea wall and up the ramp used earlier to gain access to the wall. At the top of the ramp (unless you have opted for the less strenuous alternative – see below) *turn left and follow the footpath's right bend as it climbs away from the coast. Stay with the path* (known as Middle Walk) *as it skirts the perimeter of Appley's pitch and putt course and eventually forms a junction with the sloping Appley Lane (footpath R98),* providing access to the beach (down the hill on the right). Go *straight across the lane to join a surfaced footpath (R100) running between trees (left) and the boundary wall for the grounds of St Cecilia's Abbey.*

Those disinclined to take the quite steep initial climb away from the sea wall should *turn right at the top of the ramp and retrace the outward leg of the walk past Appley Tower and back to the start point,* either ending the walk there or *walking up Appley Lane (R98) to the footpath junction and turning right onto path R100.*

The trees and bushes to the left of this footpath form the

northern boundary of land occupied by schools, the larger of which – now Bishop Lovett Middle School – was developed around St John's House, built at the end of the 1760s by Colonel (later General) William Amherst. He named it after St John's, Newfoundland, recalling his recent success in leading a British force in recapturing the strategically-important Canadian island from the French. A later owner, Edward Simeon, employed the great landscape gardener Humphry Repton to lay out the extensive grounds, which covered a far greater area than the present school limits. Rhododendrons – little known in England at the time – featured prominently. The grounds of St John's have their own ornamental tower folly, just a few feet from the footpath, which gives the impression of being a half-demolished ruin. Unlike neighbouring Appley Tower, most people pass by without knowing it's there.

Path R100 emerges at the junction of Appley Rise and Ampthill Road. Continue straight ahead, along the quietly pleasant Appley Rise, passing midway down the entrance to St Cecilia's Abbey and its Roman Catholic church (right – C on the map). The abbey owes its name to the nuns of the Community of St Cecile, who lived there from 1906 until ending their exile from France by returning there in 1922. They were quickly replaced at the Appley abbey by another group of nuns, a Benedictine community who moved there from Ventnor, and remain to this day. The abbey welcomes visitors – see details on the gate.

Continue to the thatch-covered, half-timbered (only the former is genuine!) restaurant at the foot of the road. This was built on the site of a seaside retreat – another fanciful castellated Gothic structure – built by General Amherst as part of his country estate at St John's. *Turn sharp right here to walk past the restaurant's main facade, with Ryde's boating lake* – created on land reclaimed from the sea in 1880 – *on your left. Ahead, there are short optional routes through a small area of parkland. Leaving this park, continue in the same general direction beyond the boating lake and bear right with the road as it returns you to Appley beach and the conclusion of the walk at the car park.*

WALK 13

Brading's Marshland – the remnants of a lost haven

This walk of approximately 6 miles (9.6km) passes through much of the land reclaimed from the sea through the draining of Brading Haven in the late-19th century. Most of the route, therefore, is on the flat, although there are uphill sections at both St Helens and Bembridge, neither of them particularly arduous. There are, however, a number of stiles to negotiate. Much of the route follows rural footpaths, well-defined in most cases, but some stretches of roadside walking are involved at St Helens, Bembridge and between the two on the outward leg – though this is along the harbourside Embankment Road, which has a pavement throughout.

Introduction: The reclamation of Brading Haven, flooded for centuries by the tide flowing into the Eastern Yar river, was finally achieved with the construction of the embankment between St Helens and Bembridge – concurrent with the opening of the railway branch line from Brading – in 1882. Earlier attempts, particularly in the 16th century, at holding back the sea from the main expanse of the Haven had brought only temporary success, though a great deal of the work undertaken remains remarkably intact today – and provides much of the formation for the route of the walk. The 19th century reclamation of the Haven ended for good the status of Brading as a sea port.

Parking and Public Transport: See walk 4.

Information: With much of the walk route across the marshland of the former Haven, toilet, refreshment and other facilities are concentrated at St Helens village (around the perimeter of the green) and at the Bembridge end of Embankment Road. While Brading and Bembridge are not actually on the walk route, they are easily accessible via short detours.

Directions:
Leave the station (grid ref SZ 609869 – marked A on the route

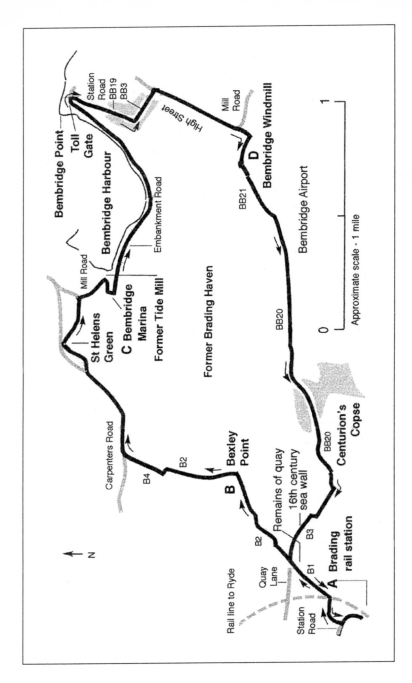

map) by walking a short distance up the approach road (Station Road) to join a path (right) between houses, indicated by a brown walk route sign. The path slopes, via barriers, to reach the end of a cul-de-sac. Carry on ahead, looking out for a second sign (right), indicating walk routes 1 and 2. Use this path between houses to pass through a metal gate and cross, with care, the rail line beyond. Turn left at the far side of the track to follow the signposted route of walk 1. Initially gravel-surfaced, the path runs alongside the rail line for a short distance before descending between hedges and veering right past water treatment works (left) as it follows the trackbed of the old Brading-Bembridge branch line.

The history of the branch line is central to the story of Brading Haven's eventual reclamation from the sea. This initial part of its route from the former junction at Brading was constructed to connect the Isle of Wight Railway's main (Ryde-Shanklin) line of 1864 with Brading's pre-reclamation quayside. In fact, although the town still enjoyed the status of an inland port as late as this, some reclamation of its haven had already been achieved – albeit for the most part temporarily. The first, simplest and entirely successful 'inning' of the haven had been accomplished in 1338. Until then the sea had encroached not only from the north-east, between St Helens and Bembridge, but also from the south-east, via Sandown Bay. Sir William Russell ended for good the latter route with the building of a causeway and bridge between his manor at Yaverland and Brading. The construction of the Yar Bridge (the area is still known as such today, though now in the form of a single word) changed the status of Yaverland-Bembridge from a tidal island of its own to a joined-up part of Wight.

In 1562 a scheme to reclaim 126.5 acres from North Marsh (north-east of the railway trackbed) was completed via a collaboration between the landowner, Sir George Oglander, of Nunwell, and Jermyn Richards, a Brading brewer who had made a fortune selling beer to the ships using the Haven – a trade not threatened by the draining of North Marsh and sufficiently profitable to have allowed him to purchase the manor of Yaverland in 1553. Jermyn's son, Edward, drained Mill Marsh and land between Yarbridge and Brading in the haven's south-west corner. Undertaken in 1594, this was particularly significant in that it provided Brading with a new quay, replacing the former, silted-up anchorage just east of the High Street. The footpath along the railway trackbed offers good views to the right across the marshland over which vessels once sailed to and from Edward Richards' quay.

Follow its winding route between trackside vegetation to reach the foot of Quay Lane at a point known in railway days as Cement Mills Crossing, a further reminder of the industrial nature of this site in bygone days. Continue the walk from here by using the narrow section of path to the left of the house ahead of you. The remains of the wall bordering the old cement works are clearly evident on the left. Bear right at the end of the narrow pathway, back on the trackbed, and then take the stile on the left to join footpath B2, signposted to St Helens. The path runs adjacent to the old rail track as it takes you over a second stile, where the directional sign indicates you are en route for Bexley Point and Carpenters Road, St Helens. The path continues on a bank, offering fine views to the left of open countryside and the downland beyond. Pass through a metal gate and follow the path, with St Helens village clearly visible ahead, over a third stile and then a fourth at Bexley Point (B on the map). Bear left here, still following the route of B2 as it runs onto an embankment.

This is part of the 16th century reclamation's seawall. The route heads due north, eventually between trees, then dips to cross a stream on a planked bridge before rising again to reach a stile at a footpath junction. Following the route of footpath B4 to Carpenters Road, indicated by the directional sign, cross the field beyond the stile, heading towards the buildings of Carpenters Farm. Pass to the right of the farm and head now in the direction of a group of cottages to reach a stile. Join the gravel-surfaced farm access track immediately beyond and walk the short distance to the bus stop at the side of Carpenters Road. The route now takes you right, alongside the road. Exercise caution as, initially, there is no continuous footway. After passing the junction with footpath B56, use the pavement for the climb into St Helens.

Bear right across the first (West) section of the expansive village green to cross St. Michael's Road and the much busier Station Road at their junctions with Upper Green Road. Continue alongside Upper Green Road for a few paces and then go diagonally across the next section of green, heading for St Helens Service Station, located at the Latimer Road-Lower Green Road junction. Cross the road here and go left along the pavement, passing the youth centre, a restaurant, the Newlands road junction and a bookshop to reach the junction with Mill Road (right). Follow this quiet lane as it

Brading and its Haven – an early-19th century pre-reclamation engraving looking towards St Helens.

descends to the western end of Bembridge Harbour, passing Old Mill Holiday Park as the road bends right near the bottom. The 18th century tide mill in question – it ceased operations in 1931 and was substantially rebuilt after the Luftwaffe wrecked the original in wartime – can be seen on the left, along with the adjacent causeway enclosing the former mill ponds. You may feel inclined to pause at the pretty, sheltered haven for small fishing and sailing vessels before *your route bears right at the water's edge and, after a few paces, takes you to a small area of new housing at Bembridge Marina. Bear right along the road, passing a tall, re-faced section of wall on the right.*

Closer investigation will reveal the wall has been here for many years and was, in fact, part of a Victorian engine shed when the marina – then known as St Helens Quay – was operated by successive railway undertakings.

More than two-and-a-half centuries before the arrival of the railway finally barred the sea from the main expanse of Brading Haven, that ambitious and, at the time, highly controversial, objective had excited the interest of the 17th century entrepreneur Sir Bevis Thelwell. Having won support for the project from King James I – who was persuaded to back it as a 'trial run' for the reclamation of the Lincolnshire fens – Thelwell engaged Sir Hugh

Myddleton, one of the most celebrated civil engineers of the era, to direct workmen from the Low Countries on the 'inning' of 700 acres – the whole of Brading Haven's still water-covered land – in 1620. Myddleton and his team had successfully dammed the mouth of the Yar at Bembridge by 1622 and for the best part of the next decade those 700 enclosed acres remained sufficiently dry to allow the experimental planting of wheat, barley, oats, cabbage-seed and rape-seed.

Only the rape flourished to any appreciable extent in the moist, sandy conditions and the whole project collapsed dramatically in 1630 when the sea breached the embankment on a March spring tide, soon rendering it beyond repair, and flooded the Haven all over again, destroying houses, farm buildings and mills in the process. The ten-year trial had cost £7,000. That might have risen by a further £4,400 some years later had an offer to repair the dam been taken up. It wasn't and, although small sections of the Haven were subsequently banked-off by various landowners, little serious interest was shown in a renewed attempt at total reclamation from the sea until the arrival of the railway age in the Victorian era.

The Brading Harbour Improvement & Railway Act of 1874 was conceived with a twin aim. It proposed, first, the building of a new embankment between St Helens and Bembridge, thus reclaiming for a second time the Haven seabed, and, second, the extension of the railway from Brading Quay – which would, of course, literally be left high and dry by the reclamation – to a new quay at St Helens and then on to a terminus at Bembridge. Financed by the decidedly shady Jabez Balfour's Liberator Building Society, the project saw thousands of tons of chalk, clay and rubble transported from pits on both sides of the Solent to form the embankment, which was equipped with sluices to control the Eastern Yar's outlet to the sea. It cost £420,000 to complete the massive project and, sadly, the lives of several workmen, who drowned when a particularly high tide smashed through the new bank. It was repaired and the embankment has defied the elements ever since.

A harbour still exists on the seaward side of the bank but it's known today as Bembridge Harbour, and Brading itself is firmly land-locked. The local sailing club's keen regard for history, however, preserves the former name of Brading Haven in its title.

Goods traffic provided the railway's first revenue. It operated as far as the new quay at St Helens from 1878 – two years before work on the embankment was concluded. There were, in fact, two quays, North and South, both equipped with sidings. You are now on the site of North Quay (C).

A short distance before the road junction ahead, turn left to walk across a bridge – marking the limit of navigation – and through the marina (C) which has replaced the railway quays to reach Embankment Road on the far side. As the name implies, the road was laid out along the top of the Victorian embankment and was operated as a railway-owned toll road until comparatively recent times. Just to the right, though out of sight across the road, is the former rail station, now a fine private residence, which still retains much of its original identity despite having seen its last train as long ago as 1953. The quayside sidings were connected to the branch line via a level crossing in Embankment Road, while the main running line of the branch continued to Bembridge on its own – still traceable – formation south of the road.

Perhaps the most remarkable feature of the quay during its railway ownership was a short-lived cross-Solent train ferry service – solely for goods traffic – to a connection with the Hayling Island branch line at Langstone Harbour. Operated by the Isle of Wight Marine Transit Company, another of the Liberator Building Society's ambitious ventures, it ran for only a short period, from August 1885 to March 1888. Its collapse was followed just a few years later by that of the notorious building society itself. The highly dubious methods resorted to by Jabez Balfour and his fellow directors to stay afloat led to litigation, arrest – though, in the case of Balfour, only after he had fled to Argentina – and, with neat irony, his eventual imprisonment in Parkhurst Prison!

Go left along Embankment Road, a fascinating harbour-side walk full of interest and character. As if awaiting the day when the tide might again break through the barrier, a diverse collection of houseboats, many of them radically modified from their sea-going days, cling defiantly to the bank, as close to the emptied Haven as possible, like a group of stranded amphibians. It's an extraordinary sight, one that for many years has been synonymous with the harbour. The yachts that reside here – notably the famous Bembridge Redwings, whose landing stages and winter quarters are passed near the harbour's eastern end, provide much of the waterborne activity today. With the embankment boasting sailing clubs at either end, the light industry south of the road is geared largely to the upkeep of their yachts.

Continue the embanked walk to Bembridge's shoreline, passing at the far end the beach-side Toll Gate Café (left), where successive railway administrations collected the tolls from motorists well into the nationalised era of British Railways – and some years beyond the closure of the rail line itself. The housing on the opposite side of the road was built on the site of the former Bembridge rail station, demolished early in the 1970s. Much more recently, the long derelict site of the Royal Spithead Hotel at the end of the road has itself been imaginatively redeveloped for residential use.

Cross the road from the café to the former station site, go left and then right with the road to take an immediate right turn into Station Road, opposite the appropriately-shaped Pilot Boat Inn. The short road – a cul-de-sac for traffic – takes you past public toilets (right – summer only) before housing gives way to woodland and the road converts into a footpath and then winds through the wood. Ignore a path ascending between houses to the left and carry on beyond an upright rail marker. With fencing now on your left, follow the path as it runs along a bank, descends via steps and takes you to a section of duck-boarding. Soon after this, bear left to climb a well-defined route (footpath BB3) to the roadside near the 'country end' of Bembridge High Street.

Go right, taking care as there is no footpath, all the way to a left-hand bend (soon after Bembridge Lodge), where the High Street becomes Mill Road. Leave the road at this point and carry on ahead, along a track providing access to Mill Farm (right) and Bembridge Windmill itself, a short distance further on (D). Built in the early 18th century, this fine example of an English 'cap' mill was in continual use until the reclamation of Brading Haven, producing flour, meal, bran and cattle feed. Output was restricted to just the cattle feed after 1897 and the mill ceased work altogether following the harvest of 1913. Used as a workshop and store by the local farmer during the First World War, the mill survived sufficiently intact to be restored in the 1930s by public subscription. It later fell again into disrepair and, after serving as a Home Guard look-out in the Second World War, mill emerged from the conflict virtually derelict. Fortunately, in 1957, Bembridge Windmill was offered by its owner to the National Trust, in whose care it has remained ever since, restored as the last functional windmill in the Isle of Wight.

Go right at the windmill to a stile and follow the route of footpath BB21, signposted to Brading, straight ahead, along the side of a field, to reach a second stile. Bear left here to cut diagonally across the next field to another stile, marked by a BB21 path directional post. Follow the signposted route down the sloping field ahead, then bear left across it to a stile and continue down a fenced-in section of path to reach another stile and footpath sign. Still following BB21, bear right here and continue the walk between a hedge (right) and fencing – beyond which, high on Culver Down in the distance, is the conspicuous monument recalling the first Lord Yarborough (Charles Pelham), founder of the Royal Yacht Squadron.

The banked path – on a further stretch of the 16th century sea defences – takes you to another stile and then onto a section that can be muddy after rain. At the next stile, the footpath sign confirms that you are now heading for Brading on path BB20 while other signs (left) warn of nearby aircraft movements at Bembridge Airport, birthplace of the famous Britten-Norman Islander light aircraft and its derivatives. *Follow the well-trodden path across the next field, then go over a stile and continue straight ahead across the field beyond and through a gap in the hedge. Still heading in the same direction, cross another field to reach a stile and stream-crossing and carry on, with the high downs west of Brading forming a backdrop to the route ahead, to cross another field, passing a lone tree. Follow the path as it turns left at the field boundary, then right and left again, as it descends to a footpath sign on the edge of Centurion's Copse. Follow the path into the copse, then bear left and climb the short distance to a path junction marked by a directional post (E).*

Combining wild beauty and peace with a hard-to-define air of dark mystery, the woodland owes its name to a corrupted form of St Urian's Copse, after an 8th century holy man, and not to the nearby Roman remains at Morton. A place abounding in legend, the copse is the site of Wolverton, most celebrated of the Island's 'lost villages,' which once flourished on the banks of Brading Haven. Wolverton was probably wiped out by the French during a 14th century attack on the Island's north-east corner, though tradition asserts that its obliteration followed the tainting of the revered St Urian's Well (spring) by the blood of a pilgrim – stoned to death by villagers who had been persuaded the innocent visitor had come deliberately to taint the water, thus triggering the catastrophic events described by a widely-believed prophecy that foretold the destruction of the place. The remains of a chapel and a nearby medieval manor were found here by Victorians.

Go *right, following the route of path BB23 as it climbs to another path junction. Turn right again, still on BB23 as it descends and bends – past a path running in from the left – to cross the Eastern Yar at Great Sluice,* constructed as part of the 16th century reclamation work. *Follow the route beyond the stile here to a second river crossing on the bridge at Middle Sluice* (another feature of the 16th century works, now designated as part of Duckers Wall). *Ignoring a path across the field to the left, maintain your direction on o a banked section of pathway.* Its impressive stone construction – easily apparent as you progress along it – reveals this as the best-preserved part of the 16th century sea wall. *Follow the path all the way to the former quayside* – still evident beneath the grass – then *bear left and right to pass through a railway 'kissing gate' to reach the old branch line trackbed again at Quay Lane. Go left and retrace your outward route back to Brading station via the railway foot crossing.*

WALK 14

Ventnor – the equitable
Island health resort

This walk combines a spectacular section of the Isle of Wight Coastal Path above rugged cliffs with a rural trek inland to the summit of Week Down. Sections of roadside walking are involved, but mostly along quiet lanes. While some of the climbing on the 4.5-mile (7.2 km) route is steep, the paths are generally well-defined and there are few stiles or potential hazards.

Introduction: Ventnor is different. South facing, it has its own 'micro climate' – reputedly the most equitable in the UK – and is protected from harsher northern influences by the highest hills on the Isle of Wight. Indeed, there is barely room for Ventnor at all between them and the English Channel. The town is built of necessity on a series of terraces, quite unlike any other part of the Island, and it was the unusual topography that delayed its emergence from the slumbers of a delightfully secluded, and little visited, fishing village – an insignificant add-on to neighbouring Bonchurch – boasting a handful of cottages, a solitary mill and the Crab & Lobster Inn. Yet, the growth of Ventnor was phenomenal once it got going. And that equitable climate was the key to it all.

Parking and Public Transport: Car parking is available (for a fee) at the Botanic Gardens, start point for the walk, on the seaward side of the A3055, a mile to the west of Ventnor and within comfortable walking distance of the town. With road instability having recently led to the closure to through traffic of the route further west – through the Undercliff – the only buses currently (2004) serving the gardens are those operating Southern Vectis local service 31 (St Lawrence-Ventnor-Wroxall).

Information: Facilities are confined to the initial coastal stretch of the walk. There are public toilets and a café at the Botanic Gardens and, by deviating for a short distance from the route at St Lawrence, the village pub and post office/shop can be visited before starting the climb up Week Down.

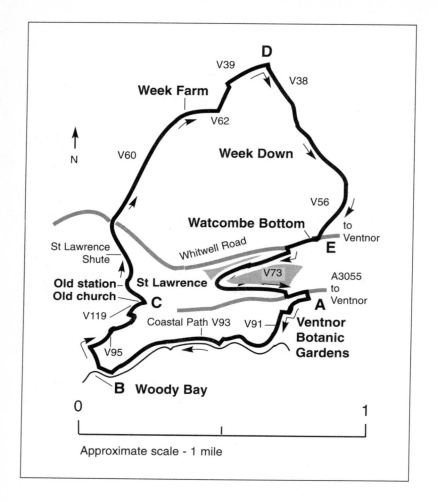

Directions:

Begin the walk at the main entrance to Ventnor Botanic Gardens (grid ref SZ 545769 – marked A on the route map). With your back to the road, go right through the top of the car park, soon passing steps (right) to a plaque explaining the origins of the gardens. The inscription records how the site of the former Royal National Hospital (1869-1964) was laid out as "a pleasure ground with special botanic interest" and was opened to the public in 1972 by Lord Mountbatten of Burma, then Governor of the Isle of Wight. But what of the earlier history?

Ventnor Cove early in the 19th century – before the town's development as a Victorian resort renowned for the health-enhancing properties of its equitable climate.

Turner may have sketched on Ventnor shore, but it was the visit in 1830 of an eminent doctor that was to play the far more significant role in transforming so dramatically the fortunes of the place. Dr (later Sir) James Clark was so struck by the health-giving properties of the mild climate and the romantically wild Undercliff just along the coast that he produced a lengthy treatise extolling its virtues. In this paper, widely read and hugely respected, Clark stressed the potential benefits of the area for patients suffering from tuberculosis and other pulmonary disorders. Ventnor became fashionable almost overnight. It developed at a pace verging on the indecent. Never mind that there was hardly any of it on the level. The terraces sprouted fine houses wherever enough land was found for them to cling to and the various residential levels were connected by a road system of Alpine proportions that still strikes a degree of terror in unsuspecting motorists – and some who actually live on the Island!

From a few hundred in the first decades of the 19th century, Ventnor's population exploded to 5,000-plus in a little over 30 years. Despite a lack of adequate links with the remainder of the Island – a situation not resolved until the Isle of Wight Railway was extended southwards from Shanklin in 1866 – it had become a coastal resort to which people not only chose to seek out in substantial numbers, but were often dispatched for the sake of their health. Three years after the railway's arrival, its 'good for your health' status was crowned with the opening of the Royal National Hospital for Diseases of the Chest – the full title of the quarter-mile long hospital that was to last for the best part of the next 100 years. Little remains today of the once extensive hospital buildings.

A small exception is soon reached as *the path along the top of the car park takes you, via toilets, past the outbuilding (right) which now houses the Island's Museum of Smuggling History,* whose fascinating exhibits are housed in vaults beneath the adjacent road. The museum is open between April and September.

The striking building housing the gardens' temperate plants is seen to the left. as you progress. For the former hospital's patients, the temperate nature of the natural climate was considered good enough – and they were constantly exposed to it! Fresh air, and plenty of it, was the order of the day when TB, unrestrained by the antibiotics in common use today, ran lethally amok among the Victorian population.

Carry on straight ahead beyond the parking area and go left with the pathway, down a slope to reach a signpost. Following the route to the Meadow and Coast Path, bear right a few paces further on to enter the Meadow, with the children's playground on your left. Bear left across the grass to another signpost and follow the route of the Coastal Path past Orchard Bay House (left) along its concrete driveway. Immediately beyond, true footpath status is adopted as the route skirts the stock fields of the Rare Breeds and Waterfowl Park (right), with a fence to the left, and takes you down to the cliffs and the start of a spectacular walk above this rugged section of the Island's coast. Walk with care as the path is very near the cliff edge and is in places devoid of clifftop hedge cover. *Stay with this well-defined route as it twists, climbs and falls – sometimes on steps – all the way to Woody Point at St Lawrence (B on the map), where it runs down via concrete steps to the cliff edge, then turns sharp right to pass between hedges and past cottages (left).*

On reaching a track, go right and climb to a 'T' junction, bearing right again up the hill (Wolverton Road – access route to

The diminutive 12th century church at St Lawrence nestles beneath
the high downs in this view from the 1880s. Church and downs
both feature on the walk route.

*the Isle of Wight Glass Studio) to reach the A3055. Cross the road,
turn left and walk the short distance to the start of signposted
footpath V119, which takes you up to St Lawrence Old Church
(C).* Essentially 12th century, though it may have Saxon origins, the
tiny church was almost certainly built as a memorial chapel for the
de Aula family. Their patron saint was St Lawrence, whose
martyrdom was assured in the 3rd century when he was burnt alive.
Until the first Earl of Yarborough, who lived nearby, extended the
chancel in 1842, this was the smallest church in England, and it still
has a strong claim to be the country's tiniest church still in regular
use. Well worth a visit, St Lawrence Old Church is generally open
between 9am and dusk.

  *Leaving the church via its entrance gate, go left, then left again
up Seven Sisters Road as far as the third turning on the right (at a
'T' junction).* The building across the road is the former St
Lawrence railway station, now a private residence. A temporary
terminus between its opening in 1897 and the line's extension to
Ventnor Town (later, more accurately re-styled as Ventnor West) in
1900, this was part of the last segment of the Island's once complex
rail network to arrive on the scene – and the first out when British
Railways axed train services in 1952. The prettiest of all the Island
railways, it was also the most hopelessly uneconomic.

Built by the nominally independent Newport, Godshill & St Lawrence Railway, but operated from the outset – and later absorbed – by the Isle of Wight Central company, it represented an attempt to entice through traffic to Ventnor via Southampton, Cowes and the Central's system southwards, rather than by the more direct route via Portsmouth, Ryde and the Isle of Wight Railway through Shanklin. It never really happened. The IWR was always the 'main line' and had the better train services – including for a period what was colloquially known as the 'Invalids' Express' which provided transport for patients heading for the Royal National Hospital. As for the competing branch line, for most of its life the route was operated as a rural byway from the country junction at Merstone. Unlike the fierce controversy surrounding later line closures on the Island, there was comparatively little in the way of local protest when the axe fell.

Go right, then left over the bridge crossing the former railway trackbed. and follow the winding road (St Lawrence Shute) as it climbs – quite steeply – to form a 'T' junction at Whitwell Road. With care, go straight across to continue the climb onto Week Down via the signposted public bridleway ahead, initially a surfaced farm roadway. Passing silos (right), continue up the concrete road between fields to reach a footpath signpost. Bear right, following the route of byway V62 for Wroxall, which climbs past cottages (left) and through the yard at Week Farm. Go through a wooden gate, alongside a larger metal farm gate, and bear left, then right , up a rough-surfaced track. On reaching a path junction, go right along the signposted route to Upper Ventnor, keeping a fence to your right as you climb steeply up the side of a field to a footpath signpost ahead – the summit of the walk (D).

Climb the stile and go right along the grassy route of path V38. Ventnor and the high downs above the town are visible to your left before the path descends towards the sea, through two gates. Ignore the stile providing access to a path on your left immediately after the second gate and continue downwards, passing further path junctions (left) and carry on ahead, now on bridleway V56, for the final section back to Whitwell road. The path passes between hedgerows and above Ventnor Rugby Club's ground (right) to emerge alongside the road at Watcombe Bottom, by a 'Welcome to Ventnor' sign (E).

Exercising caution, go right along the side of the road for 300 yards (275 metres) before crossing to the opposite side, passing through a large gap in a hedge, bearing right for a few paces and then going left, down footpath V73 (signposted to Undercliff Drive and the Botanic Gardens). The path drops between trees and bushes away from the road, with an increasingly high bank to the right. The descent is quite steep in places and further down, the path can be muddy after rain. *Stay with it beyond a path junction, bearing left to emerge at the roadside (Inglewood Park). Go left along the road until its junction with the A3055. Cross the road with care and go left along the pavement back to the botanic gardens.*

Shanklin & Sandown – the Victorian seaside

This mostly undemanding 5-mile (8km) walk recalls Victorian enterprise as it links the resorts of Sandown Bay on the Isle of Wight's 'bucket and spade' holiday coast. The outward leg from Shanklin, along an easy-to-follow, hard-surfaced section of the Island's Coastal Path, contrasts markedly with the return route via the network of rural pathways through the countryside west of the coastal conurbation. For those who prefer to do the walk in stages, direct access to the adjacent rail line is provided at both Lake and Sandown, returning you to the start of the route at Shanklin station.

Introduction: Shanklin and Sandown are both mentioned in the Domesday survey but their origins extend much further back into history. There is considerable evidence of Roman activity along the Island's eastern coastal belt. Thanks to the existence of chalybeate mineral springs in the vicinity, Shanklin was an established, if modest, resort before the accession of Queen Victoria in 1837. Sandown's importance had been principally as a military stronghold – its castle at Sandham guarding against the frequent threat of invasion by foreign forces tempted by the long, flat beach, ideal as a landing site. The invasion that was to have by far the greatest impact on both towns, however, was peaceful. It began in earnest on 23 August 1864 with the arrival of the Isle of Wight Railway from Ryde.

Parking and Public Transport: Main roads link Shanklin with all major towns on the Island. The rail station, start point for the walk, is located at the end of Regent Street, near the town centre. Parking is available at the station itself and elsewhere in the town. Frequent Island Line train services connect Shanklin with Lake, Sandown, Brading and Ryde, offering a direct interchange at Ryde Pier Head with the cross-Solent passenger ferry from Portsmouth Harbour – making this an ideal walk for day trippers travelling from the mainland. Southern Vectis bus services from all major destinations

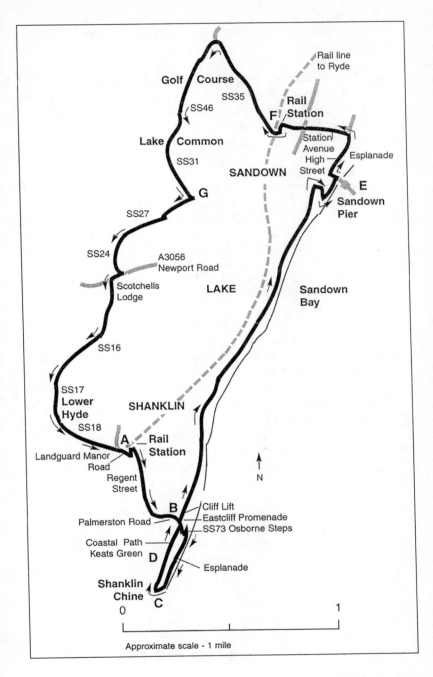

Rail line
to Ryde

Golf   Course
SS35
SS46   Rail
F   Station

Lake   Common   Station
SS31   Avenue   Esplanade
SANDOWN   High
Street

G

SS27   E
SS24   Sandown
Pier
A3056
Newport Road
Scotchells   LAKE   Sandown
Lodge   Bay

SS16

SS17
Lower
Hyde
SS18
A   Rail
Station
Landguard Manor
Road
N
Regent
Street
B   Cliff Lift
Palmerston Road   Eastcliff Promenade
SS73 Osborne Steps
Coastal Path
Keats Green   D
Esplanade
Shanklin
Chine   C
0   1

Approximate scale - 1 mile

operate to Shanklin's main stops, grouped around the Somerfield store, a short walk from the rail station.

Information: There are ample refreshment and toilet facilities on the outward leg of the walk and in the towns at either end (although some are only open during the summer season), but no direct access to facilities on the return route beyond Sandown station.

Directions:

Leaving the main entrance to Shanklin station (grid ref SZ 581818 – marked A on the route map), walk straight ahead into Regent Street and, passing St. Paul's Church (left), continue into the town centre. Ignore all turns-off to reach a 'T' junction with the High Street, opposite the town's Conservative Club. Cross the road and go up Cross Street, to the left of the club, before bearing left after a short distance into Palmerston Road. Follow this road beyond two sets of crossroads (the second at the B3328 Queens Road junction) as far as its termination at the cliff-top Eastcliff Promenade (B).

Ahead of you is the first of many glorious views across the wide expanse of Sandown Bay, sweeping round from Culver Cliff, in the far east of the Island, via the gold-tinted beaches which have lured the holidaymaking masses to the Island's east coast since the entrepreneurial Victorian era – and in 1940 persuaded Hitler seriously to consider the bay as a convenient initial landing site for a Nazi invasion of Britain.

Turn right, down the hill, and continue your own winding descent to the Esplanade below via the clearly-marked Osborne Steps (footpath SS73). Cross the road as you emerge onto the seafront to the only remaining visible reminder of Shanklin Pier – the still clearly-defined pier 'apron' bulging, to very little purpose now, from the otherwise straight lines of the promenade.

No self-respecting Victorian seaside resort was considered complete without the addition of the promenade pier. Shanklin's, extending some 1,100 feet out to sea, was opened in 1891, operated initially by troubled local enterprise, then taken over by the Urban District Council in 1899 and subsequently equipped with a central pavilion, later renewed after private enterprise resumed control in 1925. Its theatre was graced by Anna Pavlova and the Corps de Ballet in 1927 and then, over the decades that followed, by a succession of big-name entertainers. Arthur Askey, Tommy Trinder,

Jack Hylton, Cyril Fletcher, Paul Robeson . . . the names roll off the tongue. "Shanklin Pleasure Pier – The Premier Place of Amusement in the Island" roared the 1930s newspaper advertisements.

The pier had other uses. Steamers called regularly at the pier-head landing stage, and British ingenuity utilised the war-damaged structure as a 'launch-pad' for Operation PLUTO (Pipe-Line Under the Ocean) in 1944. The Victorian pier survived the threat of German invasion but, typically, its real enemy was always the natural elements.

The structure was just three years short of celebrating its centenary when it became the Island's most dramatic casualty of the hurricane that ripped through Southern England in 1988. Broken beyond repair.

Unlike the ill-fated pier, the adjacent clock tower is a Victorian survivor, having been built in 1897 to mark the Queen's Diamond Jubilee. *Continue the walk southwards (left as you face the cliffs across the road) past the clock tower* – along the first stretch of the formative 19th century seafront to be developed – *to reach the end of the Esplanade. Climb the short hill beyond, which provides access to Shanklin Chine (C),* the dramatic natural cleft where once spectacular wildness was tastefully tamed to create the town's original, and still much-visited, tourist attraction.

With the chine entrance on your left, pass through barriers onto a path which, via a sharp right turn at the Chine Inn, followed by a steep, winding section, takes you onto the undulating Keats Green section of the cliff-top Coastal Path to Sandown (D). John Keats, 'the poet's poet', vies with Alfred Lord Tennyson at the head of a highly-impressive list of 19th century literary giants with close Isle of Wight associations. The promenade now bearing his name recalls Keats' second visit to the Island in the summer of 1819. During a two-month stay on the cliffs at Eglantine Cottage, while battling against failing health, Keats wrote prodigiously – 1,500 lines of verse alone. Less than two years later, aged just 25, he was dead, 16 years before the arrival of the Victorian era, whose literature he was so greatly to influence.

George Eliot and Longfellow were notable visitors to Shanklin in the 1860s. There were many others. Their patronage helped to ensure somewhat belated fashionable status for the town. Once the opening of the rail line and improving cross-Solent communications made it much easier to reach the place, and facilities were developed to cater for residents and seasonal visitors alike, the population –

Shanklin sands – a 19th century engraving of the embryonic Victorian resort.

little more than 100 people at the end of the 18th century –
burgeoned quickly into the thousands.

*Soon rejoining Eastcliff Promenade, climb the hill, passing both
the Palmerston Road junction (left) and the cliff lift (right, opened
in 1892). Maintain your direction along the marked route of the
path until descending to reach a crossroads, with the Channel View
Hotel opposite. Following the directional signs, cross the road to
continue the route via Delphi Road straight ahead. Footpath status
is soon regained before the walk dips, then climbs past The
Hideaway café and continues on its undulating course, which offers
a magnificent coastal vista as far as Culver. Sandown Pier is
increasingly visible as the route continues past another café and the
Victorian architectural gem that is Winchester House – now a
centre for group holidays and conferences – before passing through
a green and narrowing again, now in the parish of Lake, past a
kiosk.*

Directional signs indicate that the Coastal Path (now
designated SS59) is half-a-mile from Sandown, while Lake Station
is a short walk away to the left, which may prove useful if the
weather is inclement. Lake's short-lived Victorian railway halt,
opened in 1889, was built solely to serve the adjacent County

Cricket Ground. The present station, on a different site, dates only from 1987.

The path runs onto a short section of roadway alongside houses and retirement flats. Use the pavement to climb to the next stretch of pathway, passing three large shelters (left) and an information panel (right) detailing the major cliff stabilisation work undertaken in recent years. *With the pier below now very close, descend past toilets, a caravan park and a hotel before bearing left, then right, and continuing down the sloping path. On leaving it, turn right to go down steps (immediately beyond a bench seat), then bear right at the foot of the steps to follow the route down to the seafront, emerging between the modern apartments of Napoleon's Landing (left) and public toilets (right).*

Napoleon never actually landed, of course, but the threat he posed was sufficient in itself to augment the Sandham stronghold early in the 19th century with new barracks, replaced in mid-century by accommodation bigger and better equipped (on the site now largely occupied by The Heights Leisure Centre near Lake). Soon, Sandham was surrendering, swallowed up by Victorian

Shanklin Chine, the town's original tourist attraction – a 19th century engraving of the view from the sea.

Sandown.

Turn left and walk the short distance to Sandown Pier and its range of amenities (E). Much altered over the years, the pier is the very archetype of the 'fun palace-cum-prom over the sea' – the only 'full blown' survival of the genre on the Island's coast.

There has been a pier here since 1878. Victorian Sandown extended it to 875 feet in 1895, the year the pier-head pavilion opened. Under local authority ownership, a larger pavilion was added nearer the shore-end in the 1930s. The landing stage was battered in the Second World War but later restored for the resumption of pleasure cruises. A period of partial closure in the 1970s was followed by extensive modifications which included the demolition of the old pier-head pavilion.

Celebrity entertainers drew the crowds to the modernised shore-end theatre. Jimmy Tarbuck was there in the summer of 1989, the year fire extensively damaged the rear of the building. The pier survived and it still brings in the crowds today. Though far fewer than in the years before and after World War 2, pleasure craft continue to call – notably the paddle steamer *Waverley* – but today Sandown Pier is all about providing the amusements demanded by 21st century pleasure-seekers – tenpin bowling, an all-action play area, 'adventure golf' – even an Aztec temple! The attractions may have changed but the pier is still doing what it was built to do in 1878, 'a whole day's fun in one!'

Turn left at the pier, using either the steps or pavement, to begin the short climb into Sandown High Street. Turn right and follow the town's main shopping thoroughfare as far as the fourth turn on the left (Albert Road). Use this road to gain access to Station Avenue (first left) and walk up the hill, passing (right) the former Empire Cinema and ignoring turns-off to reach the main A3055 at Broadway.

Use the pedestrian crossing (right) to continue down the remaining section of Station Avenue opposite, as far as the railway station itself (F). The impressive dimensions of the station building serve as a reminder that this was once the headquarters of the Isle of Wight Railway, The station operated as a junction between 1875 – at the peak of the Victorian railway expansion era – and 1956, when services over the cross-country route from Newport were withdrawn.

Bear left immediately before the station car park, following directions to the station entrance. Go past the entrance (opposite

Nunwell Street) and continue down Simeon Path, then onto a pathway straight ahead, away from the road as it turns into Elmbank Gardens. Turn right after a short distance to pass through a subway beneath the rail line. Cross the road immediately beyond the subway, turn right and, after a few paces, look for the sign (left) indicating the route of the Nunwell Trail (SS35) to Golf Links Road and Adgestone.

Follow the path alongside playing fields (left) as far as Fairway Athletics Centre, then continue in the same direction by using the road ahead. This is not a busy road, but exercise caution as there is no separate pathway. Beyond the entrance (right) to Fairway Holiday Park, the road bends left, then right, to pass the entrance to Sandown-Shanklin Golf Club (left). The bridleway forming the next section of the walk (initially SS46) takes you on a well-defined route through the golf course to Lake Common. The delightful rural scenery more than makes up for the need to watch out for the occasional golf ball! The route assumes more of the character of a rural pathway before emerging onto a green between houses.

At the far end (near the Lake Common road sign – G on the map) look for the sign indicating public footpath SS27 (right) to Lea Road and Blackpan. Take the climbing path the short distance into Lea Road, then turn left and, soon afterwards (alongside a children's playground), right, into Manor Road. Following the footpath directional sign (now SS26), continue straight ahead, away from the road as it bends left, on reaching Broad Lea Primary School. This section of path returns you to the countryside. Flying golf balls are no longer a consideration. The flying activity around here emanates from the nearby Isle of Wight Airport. It's all about flying for pleasure these days, but the airport did once have scheduled services to the mainland (35 minutes from Croydon to Sandown in 1951). Follow the path to a junction of routes, with a small ruined building on your right, then bear left along a track (SS24) which takes you to the A3056 Newport Road.

Turn right here and walk alongside the road, passing its junction (left) with Whitecross Lane and, further on, the Safeway store (right). Use the pedestrian crossing to reach the far side of the road and continue down it for a short distance, as far as the entrance to a track (left) alongside Scotchells Lodge.

Follow this pleasant rural route through a metal gate, up a slope and then down, ignoring the SS22 footpath turn-off (left). After a while the path bears right to cross a stream and climbs, via *a stile (or the adjacent gate), to reach a path junction at the top of the slope. The directional signs here confirm that you are on the route of byway SS17. Stay with it, following the sign to Upper Hyde, as the path takes you into the grounds of a caravan park and, soon afterwards, to a path junction. Bear left here, along bridleway SS18 (to Shanklin), and remain on this attractively wooded path as it winds its way through the park and rises, via a hard-surfaced section between fencing, to the side of Landguard Manor Road.*

Maintaining your direction, walk a short distance up the road as far as the entrance to Lower Hyde Holiday Park (right). The Isle of Wight Railway's 1866 extension southwards to Ventnor, so important in the Victorian development of the Island's south-eastern corner, formerly crossed the road here until it was controversially axed a century later – triggering a vigorous re-opening campaign that continues to the present day. *Cross the road here to the steps opposite, which lead directly to Shanklin rail station.*